CAPM Exam Prep Seminar
Participant Workbook

Published by
Instructing.com, LLC

For 35-contact hours of project management education, PDUs, or on-site training please visit: www.instructing.com.

Updated December 1, 2016; Version 5.1

Earn Your CAPM Certification

PMBOK V, PROJECTS, AND THE CAPM EXAM

CAPM Requirements

Complete application on-line

Eligibility letter from PMI

1 year from eligibility letter

Can take 3 times within one year, then wait one year to reapply

CAPM Prerequisites

Secondary degree (high school diploma, associate's degree, or the global equivalent)

And 1,500 hours of project experience

Or

Secondary degree (high school diploma, associate's degree, or the global equivalent)

And 23 hours of project management education

CAPM Exam Fees

$225 per PMI member

$300 per non-PMI member

$129 to join PMI

CAPM Exam Details

135 scored questions

15 Pretest questions

3 hours to complete the exam

Based on PMBOK Guide, fifth edition

Complete the Application Online

www.pmi.org

Can start, stop, and save your application

Complete the application ASAP – don't wait!

Certificate of Course Completion

Given at the end of the CAPM Exam Prep Seminar

Only need the certificate *if* you're audited

Complete entire course to claim application

Name on application and certificate of completion

Info to provide:
- Institution name: Instructing.com, LLC
- REP Info: #4082
- Contact hours of course: 35 contact hours
- Instructor: Joseph Phillips, CAPM

_____

_____

_____

_____

_____

_____

_____

Activity: Start Your CAPM Application

Visit www.pmi.org

Click "Certifications"

Choose Project Management Professional

Choose Apply for CAPM Certification

Apply for CAPM Certification

Register and log in to get started

APPLY NOW

ACTIVITY: CREATE A STUDY STRATEGY

STUDY TO PASS THE EXAM – NOT JUST TAKE THE EXAM

_____

_____

_____

_____

_____

_____

_____

Your Goal is to Pass the CAPM

What's your schedule like?

Can you offer one, two, or four hours every day?

My recommendation is to take the exam sooner rather than later

The longer you wait...

Complete the Course

Take the course in any order you like

Take notes as you move through the course

Review your notes before leaving a module

Ask questions! Use the discussion feature

Know What to Study

13 PMBOK Guide Chapters to Study

Real exam focus in on Chapters 4 through 13

- Integration management
- Scope
- Time
- Cost
- Quality
- Human Resources
- Communications
- Risk
- Procurement
- Stakeholders

Sample Four-Week Study Strategy

Week One: Complete the CAPM Exam Prep Seminar

Week Two:
- Module 5: Scope
- Module 6: Time
- Module 7: Cost
- Module 8: Quality
- Module 9: HR

Week Three:
- Module 10: Communications
- Module 11: Risk
- Module 12: Procurement
- Module 13: Stakeholder Management

Week Four: Put it all together
- Take all practice exams until you can score 100 percent
- Review flashcards until the are perfect every time
- Practice creating exam memory sheets

Sample Six-Week Study Strategy

Week One: Complete half of CAPM Exam Prep Seminar

Week Two: Complete remaining CAPM Exam Prep Seminar

Week Three:
- Module 5: Scope
- Module 6: Time
- Module 7: Cost

Week Four:
- Module 8: Quality
- Module 9: HR
- Module 10: Communications

Week Five:
- Module 11: Risk
- Module 12: Procurement
- Module 13: Stakeholder Management

Week Six: Put it all together
- Take all practice exams until you can score 100 percent
- Review flashcards until the are perfect every time
- Practice creating exam memory sheets

Activity: Building Your Study Strategy

Create a realistic plan
- Treat it like a project
- Schedule the work
- Execute your plan

Dedicate yourself to the project

Don't stretch this out too long

_____

_____

_____

_____

_____

_____

_____

CONSIDER THE CAPM APPLICATION AUDIT

YOUR APPLICATION COULD BE AUDITED BY PMI

Why does PMI Audit Applications?

Confirms education and experience

Enhances the credibility of the certification

Filter out "paper" project managers

CAPM Application Audit Truth

There's only one way to avoid an audit:
- Don't apply for the exam

A small percentage of applications are randomly audited

Audits are Random

You can't avoid the chance of an audit

It's random – not profiling

It's a small chance that you'll be audited

What's the audit like?

Verify education experience
- Photocopy of your degree or transcripts
- Proof of course completion

Verify project management experience
- Your project experience becomes a PDF doc
- Project supervisors will have to sign what you wrote
- Envelope also signed across the back seal

Mail all documents back to PMI Headquarters

PDUS OR CONTACT HOURS?

LEARNING THE DIFFERENCE BETWEEN THE TWO...

What is a contact hour?

Contact hours are:
- Project management education hours
- Happen before your exam application
- Must cover project management materials
- This course qualifies you for 35 contact hours

What is a PDU?

PDUs are:
- Professional Development Units
- Happen after your PMP exam
- CAPM is valid for five years
- Retake take the CAPM or move onto PMP (or other certifications)

Focus on Passing Exam, Not PDUs

Post-exam focus on PDUs

Look for my training

First things first... pass the CAPM!

UTILIZE THE COURSE RESOURCES

GETTING RESOURCES TO HELP YOUR STUDY EFFORTS

Flashcards

Create flashcards based on CAPM terms from PMBOK and other resources

Online course: flashcards provided in PDF format

Buzz through the terms every day

Knowing the terms will help you answer questions correctly

Using the Memory Sheets

Included as a resource
- PDF
- Participant workbook

You must know everything on these memory sheets

At the start of the exam recreate your memorized memory sheets

Formulas, theories, and other concepts

Participant Workbook

Follows the online course

PDF document from online course

Universal project management workbook: self-led, instructor-led, or online learning

---

Other Resources

Online course

Instructor-led course

Resources external to this course

Respect the intellectual rights of others

EXPLORE THE PMBOK GUIDE

A GUIDE TO THE PROJECT MANAGEMENT BODY OF KNOWLEDGE

_____

_____

_____

_____

_____

_____

_____

_____

1.1 Purpose of the PMBOK Guide

Generally recognized approach to project management

Describes good practice for project management

Common lexicon of project management terms

Fundamental for PMI Exams:
- CAPM
- CAPM
- PgMP
- PMI-ACP
- PMI-RMP
- PMI-SP

_____

_____

_____

_____

_____

_____

_____

All About the PMBOK Guide

A Guide to the Project Management Body of Knowledge

13 chapters

CAPM exam and the PMBOK Guide

Five process groups

47 processes

Ten knowledge areas

_____

_____

_____

_____

_____

_____

_____

PMBOK Chapters

Chapter 1: Introduction

Chapter 2: Organizational Influences and Project Life Cycle

Chapter 3: Project Management Processes – 15% of the CAPM exam

PMBOK Chapters

Chapter 4: Project Integration Management – 12% of the CAPM exam

Chapter 5: Project Scope Management – 11% of the CAPM exam

Chapter 6: Project Time Management – 12% of the CAPM exam

Chapter 7: Project Cost Management – 7% of the CAPM exam

Chapter 8: Project Quality Management – 6% of the CAPM exam

PMBOK Chapters

Chapter 9: Project Human Resource Management – 8% of the CAPM exam

Chapter 10: Project Communications Management – 6% of the CAPM exam

Chapter 11: Project Risk Management – 9% of the CAPM exam

Chapter 12: Project Procurement Management – 7% of the CAPM exam

Chapter 13: Project Stakeholder Management – 7% of the CAPM exam

Activity: Download the CAPM Assets

1. Visit www.pmi.org
2. Click Certifications
3. Choose CAPM
4. Download Exam Content Outline
5. Download Sample Questions
6. Download CAPM Handbook

CAPM Exam Guidance

Review tips, resources and FAQs to help you prepare.

Downloads

Exam Content Outline 🗎

Sample Questions 🗎

Handbook 🗎

DEFINE PROJECT BASICS

STARTING WITH A GOOD FOUNDATION OF PROJECT MANAGEMENT

1.2 What is a Project?

Temporary endeavor
- Definite beginning and end

Creates a unique product, service, or result

Projects can involve:
- A single person
- A single organizational unit
- Multiple organizational units

1.2 Projects Create…

An item, an enhancement, or a component of another item

Service or capability to perform a service

Improvement in an existing item

Result – outcome or document

1.2.1 Relationships Among Portfolios, Programs, and Projects

Coordinated, orchestrated effort for organizational goals

Strategies and prioritization

Common governance

Uniform change control

Performance measurement

1.3 What is Project Management?

Application of knowledge, skills, tools, and techniques
to meet the project requirements

47 project management processes

Five project management process groups
- Initiating
- Planning
- Executing
- Monitoring and Controlling
- Closing

1.3 Typical Project Management

Identifying requirements

Addressing needs, concerns, and expectations of stakeholders

Setting up, maintaining, and carrying out communications

Managing stakeholders

Balancing competing project constraints:
- Scope,
- Quality,
- Schedule,
- Budget,
- Resources, and Risks

1.3 Progressive Elaboration

Idea or Concept

Formulate the idea

Business Case

Feasibility Study

Project

Project Management Application Areas

Construction

Health Care

Government

Information technology

MANAGE PROJECTS AND THE ORGANIZATION

PROJECTS CAN EXIST IN MANY DIFFERENT ORGANIZATIONAL TYPES

Portfolio Management, Program Management, Project Management, and Organizational Project Management

Table 1-1 in PMBOK Guide, 5th Edition

- Scope
- Change
- Planning
- Management
- Success factors
- Monitoring

Portfolios are about maximizing return on investment

Projects, Programs, and Portfolios

Management and oversight of:
- Scope
- Changes
- Planning
- Management
- Success
- Monitoring

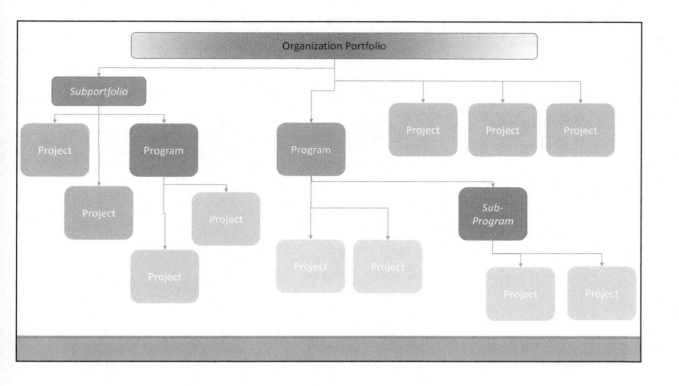

1.4.1 Program Management

Multiple related projects

Achieve benefits

Program managers and project managers

PgMP

1.4.3 Projects and Strategic Planning

Market demands

Opportunities

Social need

Environmental considerations

Customer request

Technological advance

Legal requirements

1.4.4 Project Management Offices

Support project managers

Manage shared resources across the PMO

Coaching, mentoring, and training

Conducting project audits

Developing and managing processes and procedures

Facilitating communications across projects

1.4.4 Project Management Office Types

Standards project management for an organization
- Supportive – consultative role, templates, training
- Controlling – compliance through a framework, specific forms and templates, governance
- Directive – directly manages the project as the PMO owns and controls the project life cycle

Projects and Strategic Planning

Executives — Why? Vision, Mission, Goals

Functional Management — What? Strategy and Tactics

Operations — How? LOB, Core Functions

1.5 Projects and Operations

Projects are temporary

- Developing new products or services
- Moving, Adding, Changing, or Deleting
- Implementing new service or solution

Operations are ongoing

- Repetitive actions
- Maintenance
- Core business functions

1.5 Relationship Between Projects, Operations, and Organizational Strategy

Operations and project management

Closeout or end of project phase

Product development

Improving operational processes and life cycles

Product life cycle

Knowledge transfer

1.5.2 Organizations and Project Management

Project-based organizations

Project management and organizational governance

Projects and organizational strategy

Culture

1.6 Business Value

Entire value of the business

Tangible elements
- Monetary assets
- Fixtures and equipment
- Equity

Intangible elements
- Reputation
- Brand recognition
- Trademarks

ESTABLISH THE PROJECT MANAGEMENT ROLE AND RESPONSIBILITIES

WHAT PROJECT MANAGERS DO

_____

_____

_____

_____

_____

_____

_____

1.7 Role of the Project Manager

Lead the team to achieve the project objectives

Balance the competing objectives of the project

Communicate with stakeholders

Contribute to business value

1.7.1 Responsibilities and Competencies of the Project Manager

Satisfy task needs, team needs, and individual needs

Liaison between the project team and the business strategy

Three values of a project manager:
- Knowledge: understanding project management
- Performance: accomplish as a project manager
- Personal: behavior, effectiveness, character, leadership

1.7.1 General Management Skills

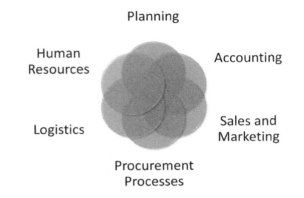

Planning

Human Resources

Accounting

Logistics

Sales and Marketing

Procurement Processes

1.7.2 Interpersonal Skills

Problem solving

Motivating

Communicating

Influencing the organization

Leadership

Negotiating

Activity: Learning Game!

http://www.instructing.com/wp-content/pub/1/story.html

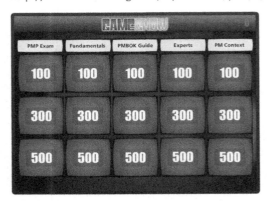

Chapter exam

_____

_____

_____

_____

_____

_____

_____

_____

ORGANIZATIONAL INFLUENCE AND PROJECT LIFE CYCLE

POWER IS INFLUENCED BY YOUR ORGANIZATIONAL STRUCTURE
& THE PROJECT LIFE CYCLE IS UNIQUE TO THE PROJECT

_____

_____

_____

_____

_____

_____

_____

2.1 Organizational Influences on Project Management

Organizational cultures and styles

Organizational communications

Structure of the organization

2.1.1 Organizational Culture

Values

Business model

Policies, methods, and processes

View of authority

Work ethic and work hours

2.1.3 Organizational Structures

Affects power of project manager

Affects decision-making abilities

Affects communication demands

Affects project team management

Affects stakeholder management

_____

_____

_____

_____

_____

_____

_____

_____

2.1.3 Organizational Structures and Project Management Power

1	Projectized
2	Strong Matrix
3	Balanced Matrix
4	Weak Matrix
5	Functional

Organizational Structures Detail

	Functional	Weak Matrix	Balanced Matrix	Strong Matrix	Projectized
Project Manager's Authority	Little	Limited	Low to Moderate	Moderate to High	High to Almost Total
Resource Availability	Little	Limited	Low to Moderate	Moderate to High	High to Almost Total
Budget Control	Functional	Functional	Mixed	Project Manager	Project Manager
Project Manager's Role	Part-time	Part-time	Full-time	Full-time	Full-time
Admin Staff	Part-time	Part-time	Part-time	Full-time	Full-time

DESCRIBE ORGANIZATIONAL FACTORS

ENTERPRISE ENVIRONMENTAL FACTORS, ORGANIZATIONAL PROCESS ASSETS, AND OTHER PROJECT ELEMENTS

2.1.4 Organizational Process Assets

Come from
- Process and procedures (historical)
- Corporate knowledge base (prepared)

Historical or prepared
- Past projects
- Lessons learned
- Processes and procedures
- Corporate knowledge base
- Guidelines and accepted practices

2.1.4.2 Corporate Knowledge Base

Configuration management knowledge

Financial databases: labor hours, incurred costs, budgets, and any project cost overruns;

Historical information and lessons learned knowledge bases

Issue and defect management databases

Process measurement databases

Project files from previous projects

2.1.5 Enterprise Environmental Factors

Organizational policies

Industry standards and regulations

Rules that the project manager must abide by

Processes that must be followed

Geographic distribution of facilities

Marketplace conditions

Standards and Regulations

Standards are optional

Regulations are not

2.2 Project Stakeholders and Governance

Interested parties in the project's existence

Affected by the project

Can affect the project

Project team

Project manager

2.2.1 Project Stakeholders

Anyone who's affected by the project

Positive stakeholders

Negative stakeholders

Neutral stakeholders

2.2.1 Project Stakeholders

Common stakeholders
- Sponsor
- Customers and users
- Sellers
- Business partners
- Organizational groups
- Functional managers

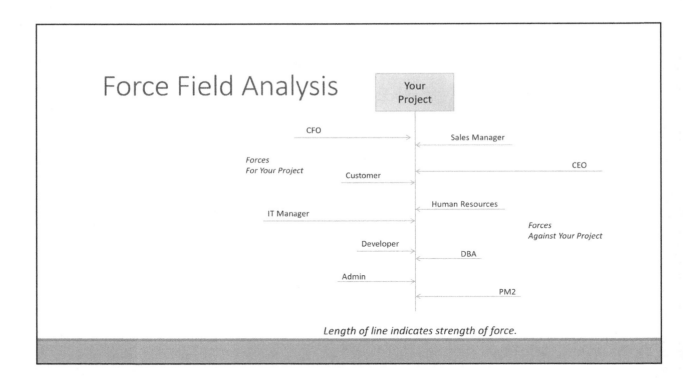

2.2.2 Project Governance

Deliverable acceptance criteria

Escalation process

Relationship among projects, programs, project team, stakeholders

Process for communicating information

Decision-making process

Project life cycle approach

Process for stage gate or phase reviews

Control and oversight of the project

_____

_____

_____

_____

_____

_____

_____

9.3.2.4 Establishing Ground Rules

Once the ground rules have been established, it's the responsibility of the entire project team to enforce the rules.

2.2.3 Project Success

Define what equates to project success first

Meeting project objectives
- Scope
- Costs
- Schedule
- Quality
- Resources
- Risk

2.3 Project Team

Dedicated – project team works on the project full time
- Collocated or virtual
- Reports directly to project manager
- Lines of authority are clear

Part-time – project team works part time on the project
- Carries on regular operational work
- Functional manager usually in control of project resources
- Project team could be on multiple projects at one time

PROJECT LIFE CYCLE

PROJECTS HAVE A UNIQUE LIFE CYCLE

_____

_____

_____

_____

_____

_____

_____

2.4 Project Life Cycle

Unique to each project

Duration of the project

Phases

Phases of construction versus phases of IT projects

Concept → Design → Drawings → Bid → Construction

2.4.2 Project Phases

Phases result in key deliverables

Phase names describe work:
- Foundation
- Framing
- Interior
- Exterior

Milestones often linked to phases

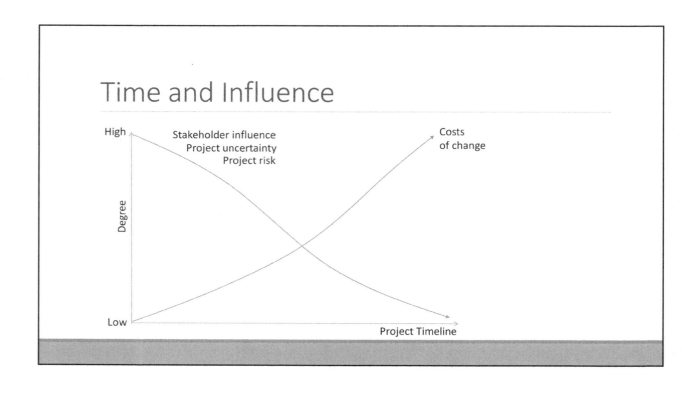

2.4 Product and Project Life Cycles

Life of the product

Last product phase is its retirement

Project life cycle typically does one of these activities (MACD):
- Moving
- Adding
- Changing
- Deleting

_____

_____

_____

_____

_____

_____

_____

2.4.2.1 Project Phase Relationships

Sequential relationship

Overlapping relationship

Iterative relationship

2.4.2.2 Predictive Life Cycles

Plan-driven

Waterfall approach

Predicts the project life cycle

Changes to scope are tightly controlled

2.4.2.3 Iterative and Incremental Life Cycles

Phases repeat through iterations

Iterations create deliverables

Detailed scope is elaborated for each iteration

Changes to the project scope are expected

2.4.2.4 Adaptive Life Cycles

Change-driven

Agile project management

Rapid iterations or project work

Backlog of requirements

Changes to the project scope are expected

_____

_____

_____

_____

_____

_____

_____

Learning Game!

http://www.instructing.com/wp-content/pub/2/story.html

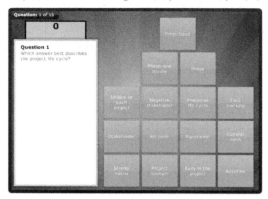

Chapter exam

EXPLORE PROJECT MANAGEMENT PROCESSES

47 PROJECT MANAGEMENT PROCESSES

_____

_____

_____

_____

_____

_____

_____

Project and Product Processes

Project management processes – flow of the project

Product processes – specify and create the project's product
- Vary by application area
- Execution of the project work
- Project scope defines the product
  - Construction
  - Computer programming
  - Network Infrastructure
  - Designing a web site

Project Management Processes

What is a process?
- Set of interrelated actions and activities
- Create a pre-specified result

Five groups of processes

47 project management processes

Inputs, Tools and Techniques, Outputs

Project Success Depends on...

- Use the most appropriate processes
- Use a defined and documented approach
- Comply with stakeholder requirements
- Balance time, cost, scope, quality, and risk

3.1 Project Management Processes

Apply globally across industries

You should not apply every process

Use the most appropriate processes

Depth of execution for each process used

Project Management Process Groups

Initiating

Planning

Executing

Monitoring and Controlling

Closing

WALK-THROUGH INITIATING PROCESSES

THERE ARE 2 INITIATING PROCESSES.

3.3 Initiating Process Group

Two processes:
- Develop project charter
- Identify stakeholders

ANALYZE
PLANNING PROCESSES

THERE ARE 24 PLANNING PROCESSES.

_____

_____

_____

_____

_____

_____

_____

_____

3.4 Planning Process Group

24 processes:
- Develop project management plan
- Plan scope management
- Collect requirements
- Define scope
- Create work breakdown structure
- Plan schedule management
- Define activities

3.4 Planning Process Group

24 processes, continued:

- Sequence activities
- Estimate activity resources
- Estimate activity durations
- Develop schedule
- Plan cost management
- Estimate costs
- Determine budget

3.4 Planning Process Group

24 processes, continued:
- Plan quality management
- Plan human resource management
- Plan communications
- Plan risk management
- Identify risks
- Perform qualitative analysis
- Perform quantitative analysis

3.4 Planning Process Group

24 processes, continued:
- Plan risk responses
- Plan procurement management
- Plan stakeholder management

SURVEY
EXECUTING PROCESSES

THERE ARE 8 EXECUTING PROCESSES.

3.5 Executing Process Group

Eight processes
- Direct and manage project work
- Quality assurance
- Acquire project team
- Develop project team
- Manage project team
- Manage communications
- Conduct procurement
- Manage stakeholder engagement

REVIEW MONITORING AND CONTROLLING PROCESSES

THERE ARE 11 MONITORING AND CONTROLLING PROCESSES.

_____

_____

_____

_____

_____

_____

_____

_____

3.6 Monitoring and Controlling Process Group

11 processes
- Monitor and control project work
- Integrated change control
- Validate scope
- Control scope
- Control schedule

3.6 Monitoring and Controlling Process Group

11 processes, continued
- Control costs
- Control quality
- Control communications
- Control risks
- Control procurements
- Control stakeholder engagement

_____

_____

_____

_____

_____

_____

_____

COMPLETE CLOSING PROCESSES

THERE ARE 2 CLOSING PROCESSES.

3.7 Closing Process Group

Two processes
- Close project or phase
- Close procurement

WORK WITH PROJECT PROCESSES

PROJECT EVENTS DETERMINE WHICH PROCESS TO UTILIZE

3.8 Project Information

Work performance data – raw observation and measurements
- ◦ Percent of work completed
- ◦ Actual start and finish dates for activities
- ◦ Number of change requests, defects, actual costs

Work performance information – data that has been analyzed
- ◦ Status of deliverables
- ◦ Implementation status for change requests
- ◦ Forecasts for estimate to complete

Work performance reports – reports that communicate the work performance information

3.9 Role of the Knowledge Areas

Ten project management knowledge areas:
- Project integration management
- Project scope management
- Project cost management
- Project schedule management
- Project quality management
- Project human resource management
- Project communications management
- Project risk management
- Project procurement management
- Project stakeholder management

Learning Game!

http://www.instructing.com/wp-content/pub/3/story.html

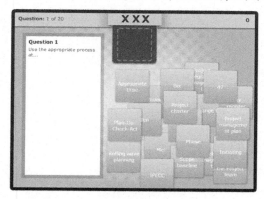

Chapter exam

MASTER PROJECT INTEGRATION MANAGEMENT

ACTIONS IN ONE AREA OF THE PROJECT AFFECT ALL OTHER AREAS OF THE PROJECT

_____

_____

_____

_____

_____

_____

_____

Choosing a Project

Opportunities

Problems

Customer request

Benefits Measurement

Compare the benefits of the project

Cost-benefits ratio

Scoring models

Murder boards

Payback period

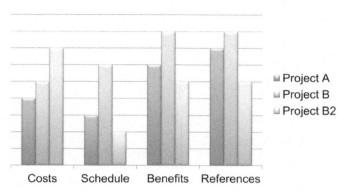

Project A
Project B
Project B2

Costs   Schedule   Benefits   References

Future Value of Money

$FV = PV(1+i)^n$ where:

- FV is future value
- PV is present value
- i is the given interest rate
- n is the number of time periods

Future Value of Money

$FV=PV(1+i)^n$

- PV is $100,000
- i is .06
- n is five years

Future Value of Money

FV=PV$(1+i)n$

- PV is $100,000
- i is .06
- n is five years

FV=100,000$(1.06)5$

- FV=100,000(1.338226)
- FV=133,822.60

Present Value of Money

PV=FV/$(1+i)^n$

- PV is present value
- FV is future value
- i is the given interest rate
- n is the number of time periods

Present Value of Money

$PV = FV/(1+i)^n$

- FV is $160,000
- i is .06
- n is five years

$PV = 160{,}000/(1.338226)$

$PV = \$119{,}561$

Net Present Value

Finds the true value of a project

Considers a project with multiple returns

Considers the initial cash outlay

Net Present Value

Calculate the return for each time period

Calculate each time period's present value

Sum the present value

Subtract the investment

NPV greater than zero is good

Net Present Value

Time Period	Cash Flow	Present Value
1	$15,000	$14,150.94
2	$25,000	$22,249.91
3	$17,000	$14,273.53
4	$25,000	$19,802.34
5	$18,000	$13,450.65
Totals	$100,000	$83,927.37
Investments		$78,000.00
Net Present Value		$5,927.37

Internal Rate of Return

Present value equals cash inflow

IRR with higher values are good

IRR with lower values might be poor

LAUNCH A NEW PROJECT

EXAMINING THE DOCUMENTS FOR NEW PROJECTS

_____

_____

_____

_____

_____

_____

_____

_____

4.1 Develop Project Charter

Authorized external to the project

Appropriate power

Portfolio Steering Committee

ITTO: Develop Project Charter

Inputs	Tools & Techniques	Outputs
Project statement of work	Expert judgment	Project charter
Business case	Facilitation techniques	
Agreements		
Enterprise environmental factors		
Organizational process assets		

4.1.1.1 Project Statement of Work

Business need

Product scope description

Strategic plan

4.1.1.2 Examining the Business Case

Determines worth of the project

Justifies the investment

Created as a result of:
- Market demand
- Organizational need
- Customer request
- Technological advance
- Legal requirement
- Ecological impacts
- Social need

4.1.2 Creating the Project Charter

Expert judgment
- Consultants
- Internal organizational resources
- Stakeholders
- Industry groups
- PMO

Facilitation techniques
- Brainstorming
- Conflict resolution
- Meeting management

Developing the Project Charter

Requirements for satisfaction

Approval requirements

Project manager

Project sponsor

High-level purpose of the project

Developing the Project Charter

Purpose of the project

Milestone schedule

Stakeholder influence

Risks

Developing the Project Charter

Functional organizations

Summary budget

Contract

PLAN THE PROJECT

PLANNING IS AN ITERATIVE ACTIVITY THROUGHOUT THE PROJECT.

ITTO: Develop Project Management Plan

Inputs	Tools & Techniques	Outputs
Project charter	Expert judgment	Project management plan
Outputs from other processes	Facilitation techniques	
Enterprise environmental factors		
Organizational process assets		

Purpose for the Plan

- Communicates intent of the project
- Serves as a guide for the project manager
- Provides project structure
- Provides documentation
- Provides baselines

Developing the Project Plan

Triple Constraints of Project Management

Iron Triangle

Balance time, cost, and scope constraints

Planning Participants

Participant	Contribution
Project manager	Leadership, facilitation, organization, direction, expert judgment
Project team members	Knowledge of project work, time estimating, schedule, risk assessment, expert judgment
Customers	Objectives, quality requirements, influence on budget and schedule
Management	Budget, resources, project management methodology, quality requirements, project plan approval

Typical Project Management Plan

Change management plan	Scope baseline
Communications management plan	Quality management plan
Configuration management plan	Requirements management plan
Cost baseline	Risk management plan
Cost management plan	Schedule baseline
HR management plan	Schedule management plan
Process improvement plan	Scope management plan
Procurement management plan	Stakeholder management plan

Activity attributes	Activity cost estimates	Activity duration estimates	Activity list
Activity resource requirements	Agreements	Basis of estimates	Change log
Change requests	Forecasts (costs, schedule)	Procurement documents	Procurement statement of work
Issue log	Milestone list	Project funding requirements	Project schedule
Project calendars	Project charter	Project statement of work	Quality checklists
Project schedule network diagrams	Project staff assignments	Requirements documentation	Requirements traceability matrix
Quality control measurements	Quality metrics	Risk register	Schedule data
Resource breakdown structure	Resource calendars	Stakeholder register	Team performance assessments
Seller proposals	Source selection criteria	Work performance reports	Work performance data
Work performance information			

EXECUTE THE PROJECT PLANS

PROJECT MANAGEMENT IS ABOUT GETTING THINGS DONE.

_____

_____

_____

_____

_____

_____

_____

4.3 Direct and Manage Project Work

Doing the work to satisfy the project objectives

Spending funds to satisfy the project objectives

Managing, training, and leading the project team

Completing procurement requirements

Managing sellers

Acquiring, managing, and using resources such as materials, tools, facilities, and equipment to get the project work completed

4.3 Direct and Manage Project Work

Managing risks

Fleshing approved changes into the project

Managing communications

Collecting project data on schedules, costs, quality, and overall project progress—and then reporting on these components

Completing lessons learned documentation

Managing stakeholder engagement

_____

_____

_____

_____

_____

_____

_____

_____

ITTO: Direct and Manage Project Work

Inputs	Tools & Techniques	Outputs
Project management plan	Expert judgment	Deliverables
Approved change requests	Project management information system	Work performance data
Enterprise environmental factors	Meetings	Change requests
Organizational process assets		Project management plan updates
		Project documents updates

Actions in Execution

Corrective action – realigns project performance

Preventive action – ensures future performance

Defect repair – modifies nonconformance to project requirements

These actions usually require a change request

Corrective Actions

 **Fixing the project**

 **Defect repair**

 **Defect repair validation**

Preventive Actions

Safety

Training

Anticipated problems

Risk management

MONITOR AND CONTROL THE PROJECT

MONITORING AND CONTROLLING HAPPENS IN TANDEM WITH PROJECT EXECUTION

4.4 Monitor and Control Project Work

Compare actual experiences to project management plan

Assess project performance

Identify new risks

Maintain information about the project's current state

ITTO: Monitor and Control Project Work

Inputs	Tools & Techniques	Outputs
Project management plan	Expert judgment	Change requests
Schedule forecasts	Analytical techniques	Work performance reports
Cost forecasts	Project management information system	Project management plan updates
Validated changes	Meetings	Project documents updates
Work performance information		
Enterprise environmental factors		
Organizational process assets		

Enterprise Environmental Factors

Government and industry standards

Company work authorization system

Risk tolerances

PMIS

Organizational Process Assets

Communication requirements

Financial control procedures

Issue and defect management procedures

Change control procedures

Risk control procedures

Process measurement database

Lessons learned database

Forecasting Project Performance

Schedule forecasts
- Estimate to complete
- Schedule variance
- Schedule performance index

Costs forecasts
- Estimate to complete
- Estimate at completion
- Cost variance
- Cost performance index

PERFORM INTEGRATED CHANGE CONTROL

CHANGE CAN AFFECT THE ENTIRE PROJECT

4.5 Perform Integrated Change Control

Ensure only approved changes

Review change requests promptly

Manage approved changes

Maintain baselines

Review, approve, or decline change requests

Coordinate changes across project

Document change request and impact

_____

_____

_____

_____

_____

_____

_____

ITTO: Perform Integrated Change Control

Inputs	Tools & Techniques	Outputs
Project management plan	Expert judgment	Approved change requests
Work performance reports	Meetings	Change log
Change requests	Change control tools	Project management plan updates
Enterprise environmental factors		Project documents updates
Organizational process assets		

Configuration Control

Specification the deliverables and the processes

Features and functions

How the project work is completed

Configuration Control

Configuration identification – identification and documentation of the product and its components

Configuration status accounting – includes the documentation of the product information

Configuration verification and auditing – concerned with performance and functional attributes of the product

Managing Project Change

- Documented change requests
- Unapproved changes
- Scope creep
- Gold plating

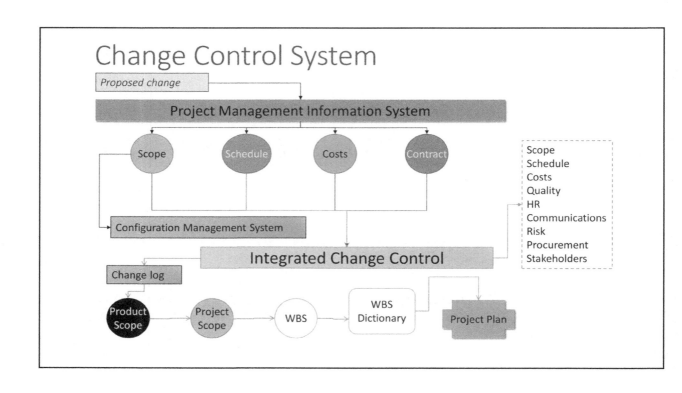

CLOSE THE PROJECT

CLOSING IS THE HAPPIEST DAY OF THE PROJECT

_____

_____

_____

_____

_____

_____

_____

4.6 Close Project or Phase

Contract documentation

Enterprise environmental factors

Work performance information

Deliverables

Preparing to archive

ITTO: Close Project or Phase

Inputs	Tools & Techniques	Outputs
Project management plan	Expert judgment	Final product, service, or result transition
Accepted deliverables	Analytical techniques	Organizational process assets updates
Organizational process assets	Meetings	

Closing the Project

Assembling project records

Project success or failure

Lessons learned documentation

Archiving the records

Learning Game!

http://www.instructing.com/wp-content/pub/4/story.html

Chapter exam

PLAN PROJECT SCOPE MANAGEMENT

MANAGING ALL OF THE REQUIRED WORK – AND ONLY
THE REQUIRED WORK

5.1 Planning Scope Management

Creates the scope management plan to:
- Documents scope definition process
- Scope validation process
- Scope control process

Offer direction for scope management

Helps combat scope creep

_____

_____

_____

_____

_____

_____

_____

ITTO: Planning Scope Management

Inputs	Tools & Techniques	Outputs
Project management plan	Expert judgment	Scope management plan
Project charter	Meetings	Requirements management plan
Enterprise environmental factors		
Organizational process assets		

Project and Product Scope

Product scope – features and functions

Project scope – work to be completed

COLLECT PROJECT REQUIREMENTS

REQUIREMENTS ARE WHAT THE PROJECT MUST ADHERE TO AND
DELIVER FOR THE PROJECT TO BE SUCCESSFUL

_____

_____

_____

_____

_____

_____

_____

_____

5.2 Collect Requirements

Business requirements: higher-level needs of the organization

Stakeholder requirements: needs of a stakeholder or stakeholder group

Solution requirements: features, functions, and characteristics of the product, service
- Functional requirements describe the behaviors of the product.
- Nonfunctional requirements describe the environmental conditions or qualities

Transition requirements: moving from the current state to the future state.

Project requirements: actions, processes, or other conditions

Quality requirements: criteria needed to validate the successful completion of a project deliverable or fulfillment of other project requirements

ITTO: Collect Requirements

Inputs	Tools & Techniques	Outputs
Scope management plan	Interviews	Requirements documentation
Requirements management plan	Focus groups	Requirements traceability matrix
Stakeholder management plan	Facilitated workshops	
Project charter	Group creativity techniques	
Stakeholder register	Group decision-making techniques	
	Questionnaires and surveys	
	Observations	
	Prototypes	
	Benchmarking	
	Context diagrams	
	Document analysis	

Interviewing Stakeholders

Stakeholder register

One-to-one

One-to-many

Many-to-many

Focus Groups

Moderated event

6-12 people

Neutral moderator

Participant composition

Facilitated Workshop

Requirements workshop

Commonality, consensus, cohesion

Joint application design workshop

Voice of the customer

Quality function deployment

Group Creativity Techniques

Brainstorming

Nominal group technique

Mind mapping

Affinity diagram

Delphi Techniques

Survey One Broad

Survey Two More specific

Survey Three

Survey Four

Delphi technique

Using Group Decisions

Unanimity – everyone agrees

Majority – more than 50 percent agrees

Plurality – largest block agrees

Dictatorship – power decides

Questionnaires and Surveys

Large group

Paper-based

Web-based

Geographical concerns

Stakeholder Observation

Job shadowing

Passive

Active (participant observer)

Prototypes

Throw-away prototypes

Functional prototypes

Storyboarding

Benchmarking the Requirements

Comparing two or more system, businesses, approaches

Set an external basis for performance

Comparing organizations for requirements

Utilizing a Context Diagram

Scope model

Business system working components
- Servers
- Workstations
- Databases
- Workflow
- People (actors)

Analyzing Project Documents

Project plans

Brochures

Blueprints

Specifications

_____

_____

_____

_____

_____

_____

_____

Managing the Project Requirements

Requirements Traceability Matrix
- Table of requirements
- Business needs
- Project objectives
- WBS deliverables
- Product components
- Development
- Related test cases

DEFINE THE PROJECT SCOPE

THE PROJECT SCOPE STATEMENT DEFINES THE OBJECTIVES OF THE PROJECT ENDEAVOR

5.3 Define Scope

Detailed description the project and the product

Project boundaries

Project scope statement

Scope baseline
- Project scope statement
- Project WBS
- Project WBS dictionary

ITTO: Define Scope

Inputs	Tools & Techniques	Outputs
Scope management plan	Expert judgment	Project scope statement
Project charter	Product analysis	Project documents updates
Requirements documentation	Alternatives generation	
Organizational process assets	Facilitated workshops	

Defining the Project Scope

Expert judgment
- Consultants
- Stakeholders, including customers
- Professional and technical associations
- Industry groups
- Subject matter experts

Product Analysis

Product breakdown

Systems engineering

Value engineering

Value analysis

Function analysis

Quality function deployment

Alternatives Generation

Benchmarking

Systems

Vendors

Materials

Resources

Facilitated Workshops

Stakeholder expectations

Documentation

Communication

Verification

Business analysts

Examining a Project Scope Statement

Product scope description

Product acceptance criteria

Project deliverables

Project exclusions

Project constraints

Project assumptions

Project Charter versus Project Scope

Project Charter
- Project purpose or justification
- Measurable project objectives
- High-level requirements
- High-level project description
- High-level risks
- Summary milestone schedule
- Summary budget
- Stakeholder list
- Project approval requirements
- Assigned project manager, responsibility, and authority level
- Name and authority of the sponsor

Project Scope
- Project scope description
- Acceptance criteria
- Project deliverables
- Project exclusions
- Project constraints
- Project assumptions

Project Scope Statement Updated Docs

Stakeholder register

Requirements documentation

Requirements traceability matrix

CREATE THE WBS

THE WORK BREAKDOWN STRUCTURE IS A DECOMPOSITION OF THE PROJECT SCOPE

5.4 Create WBS

Process of decomposing the project scope

Deliverables-orientated

Not the activities list

Major component of the scope baseline

Project planning tools

Visualizes the project

Defines what's in scope

Deterrent to scope change

ITTO: Create WBS

Inputs	Tools & Techniques	Outputs
Scope management plan	Decomposition	Scope baseline
Project scope statement	Expert judgment	Project documents updates
Requirements documentation		
Enterprise environmental factors		
Organizational process assets		

WBS Creation

Major project deliverables identified

Structure and organize the WBS

Decompose upper-level components to lower-level components

Assigning identification codes to components

Verify the scope decomposition

Finalizing the WBS

Control accounts for work packages

Code of accounts - unique identifier

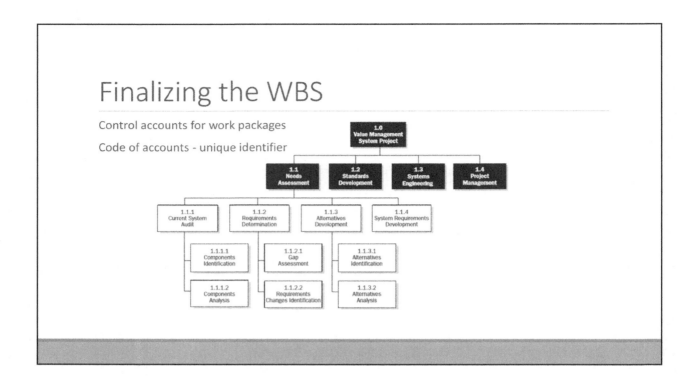

WBS Templates

Historical information

Pre-populated deliverables

Sometimes called a WBT

WBS Dictionary

Defines all elements of the WBS

Defines work package attributes

Time, cost, requirements, resources

Follows WBS usage

WBS Dictionary includes:

- Code of account identifier
- Description of work
- Assumptions and constraints
- Responsible organization
- List of schedule milestone
- Associated schedule activities

- Resources required
- Cost estimates
- Quality requirements
- Acceptance criteria
- Technical references
- Contract information

Scope Baseline

Project scope statement

WBS

WBS Dictionary

VALIDATE PROJECT SCOPE

SCOPE VALIDATION LEADS TO CUSTOMER ACCEPTANCE OF THE PROJECT WORK

_____

_____

_____

_____

_____

_____

_____

5.5 Validate Scope

Inspection-driven process

Customer inspects the project work

Phase and project completion

Review, audits, walkthroughs

Leads to formal project acceptance

ITTO: Validate Scope

Inputs	Tools & Techniques	Outputs
Project management plan	Inspection	Accepted deliverables
Requirements documentation	Group decision-making techniques	Change requests
Requirements traceability matrix		Work performance information
Verified deliverables		Project documents updates.
Work performance data		

Inspecting the Project Work

Measuring

Examining

Testing

Validating

Reviews

Walk-throughs

Audits

Formally Accepting the Project Work

Accepted deliverables for phases and the project

Sign-off of deliverables

Change requests are a possible output

Scope validation and quality control

CONTROL THE PROJECT SCOPE

YOU MUST CONTROL THE PROJECT SCOPE TO ENSURE THAT YOU'RE DELIVERING EXACTLY WHAT THE CUSTOMER HAS REQUESTED

5.6 Control Scope

Are changes agreed upon?

Has the change already happened?

How to manage the existing change?

How to incorporate approved changes?

What baselines are affected by the change?

ITTO: Control Scope

Inputs	Tools & Techniques	Outputs
Project management plan	Variance analysis	Work performance information
Requirements documentation		Change requests
Requirements traceability matrix		Project management plan updates
Work performance data		Project documents updates
Organizational process assets		Organizational process assets updates

Variance Analysis

Performance measurements

Magnitude of variation

Determine cause and degree of variance

Corrective or preventive action

Updating the Scope Statement

Change affects the project scope statement

Versioning is appropriate

Approved changes affect the scope baseline

Could affect cost and schedule baselines

Learning Game!

http://www.instructing.com/wp-content/pub/5/story.html

Chapter exam

_____

_____

_____

_____

_____

_____

_____

PLAN SCHEDULE MANAGEMENT

PLANNING, ESTIMATING, SCHEDULING, AND CONTROLLING THE PROJECT WORK TO FINISH ON TIME

6.1 Plan Schedule Management

Defines how the schedule will be:
- Developed
- Managed
- Executed
- Controlled

Defines schedule management approach for entire project

ITTO: Plan Schedule Management

Inputs	Tools & Techniques	Outputs
Project management plan	Expert judgment	Schedule management plan
Project charter	Analytical techniques	
Enterprise environmental factors	Meetings	
Organizational process assets		

What's in the Schedule Management Plan?

Schedule management plan includes:
- Project schedule model development
- Level of accuracy
- Units of measure (hours, days, weeks)
- Organizational procedure links
- Project schedule model maintenance
- Control thresholds
- Rules for performance measurements
- Reporting formats
- Process descriptions

_____

_____

_____

_____

_____

_____

_____

_____

DEFINE THE PROJECT ACTIVITIES

ACTIVITIES CREATE THE ELEMENTS WITHIN THE PROJECT'S WORK BREAKDOWN STRUCTURE

_____

_____

_____

_____

_____

_____

_____

_____

6.2 Define Activities

Activities associated with work packages

Basis for estimating, scheduling, and controlling work

Activities list

Activity attributes

Milestone list

ITTO: Define Activities

Inputs	Tools & Techniques	Outputs
Schedule management plan	Decomposition	Activity list
Scope baseline	Rolling wave planning	Activity attributes
Enterprise environmental factors	Expert judgment	Milestone list
Organizational process assets		

Defining the Project Activities

Project work and project manager work

Planning processes

Sequence of activities

Procurement time

Internal and external events

Known and unknown events

Decompose Project Activities

Activity list and work packages

8/80 Rule

Requires three inputs:
- Scope baseline
- Enterprise environmental factors
- Organizational process assets

Activity List

Separate document

Lists all project activities

Activity identifier

Scope of work description

Rolling Wave Planning

Imminent work versus distant work

Phase gate planning

Iterations of planning

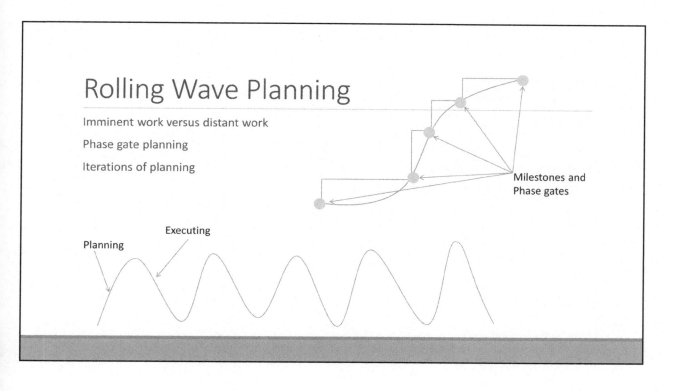

Templates

Historical information

Pre-populated forms and plans

Organizational process assets

Planning Components

Control accounts
- Management control point
- Scope, cost, and schedule
- Performance measurement

Planning packages
- Decisions to be completed
- Issues

Activity Attributes

Activity name and description

Activity ID

WBS identifier

Relationships

Leads and lags

Activity Attributes

Resource requirements

Imposed dates

Constraints and assumptions

Additional information

SEQUENCE THE PROJECT ACTIVITIES

SEQUENCE THE ACTIVITIES IN THE BEST ORDER TO REACH THE END OF THE PROJECT

6.3 Sequence Activities

Computer-driven

Manual process

Blended approach

Predecessors and successors

Milestone list

ITTO: Sequence Activities

Inputs	Tools & Techniques	Outputs
Schedule management plan	Precedence diagramming method (PDM)	Project schedule network diagrams
Activity list	Dependency determination	Project documents updates
Activity attributes	Leads and lags	
Milestone list		
Project scope statement		
Enterprise environmental factors		
Organizational process assets		

Precedence Diagramming Method

Finish-to-Start

Start-to-Start

Finish-to-Finish

Start-to-Finish

Dependency Determination

Mandatory dependencies – hard logic

Discretionary dependencies – soft logic

External dependencies – external constraint

Internal dependencies – type of hard logic

Leads and Lags

Lead is accelerated time

Lead allows activities to overlap

Lag is waiting time

Lag moves activities farther apart

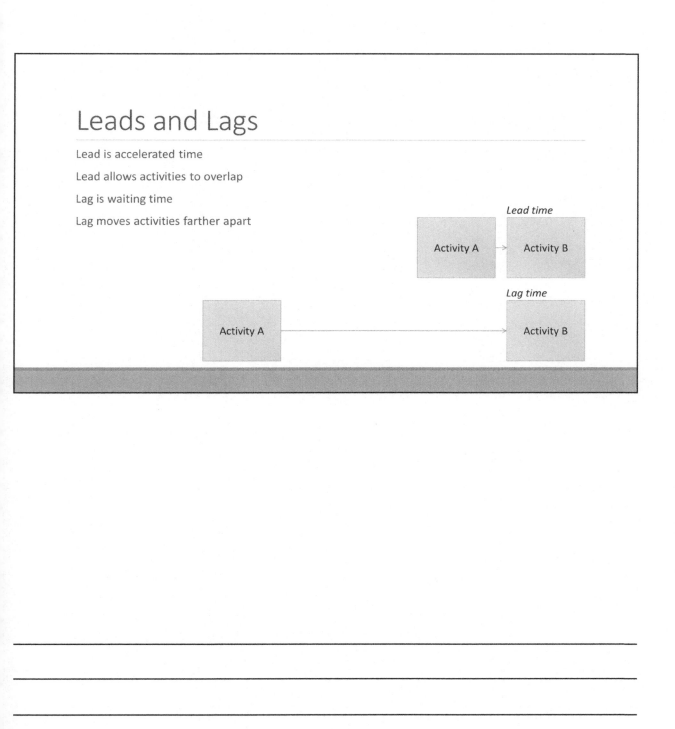

Network Templates

Previous projects

Pre-populated templates

Organizational process assets

Sequencing Outputs

Required work should be scheduled

Finish-to-start relationship most common

Activity sequence is not the schedule

PERT charts aren't PNDs

Updating the PND

Changes to the project scope

Updates to the scope baseline

Updates to the activities list

Updates to the PND

ESTIMATE THE ACTIVITY RESOURCES

ACTIVITIES WILL NEED PEOPLE, EQUIPMENT, TOOLS, FACILITIES AND
MATERIALS IN ORDER TO BE COMPLETE

_____

_____

_____

_____

_____

_____

_____

6.4 Estimate Activity Resources

Resources to complete activities
- People
- Equipment
- Materials
- Facilities

ITTO: Estimate Activity Resources

Inputs	Tools & Techniques	Outputs
Schedule management plan	Expert judgment	Activity resource requirements
Activity list	Alternative analysis	Resource breakdown structure
Activity attributes	Published estimating data	Project documents updates
Resource calendars	Bottom-up estimating	
Risk register	Project management software	
Activity cost estimates		
Enterprise environmental factors		
Organizational process assets		

Resource Availability

Resource calendar

Negotiate for resources

Move the related activity

Delay the activity or project

Find alternative resources

Activity Resource Needs

Effort-driven activities

Fixed-duration activities

Effort can affect completion date

Law of Diminishing Returns

Examining Project Calendars

Project calendar – when the project work takes places

Resource calendar – when resources are available

Creating a Resource Breakdown Structure

Like the WBS

Utilization of resources

Expose resource constraints

Identify resource needs

ESTIMATE THE ACTIVITY DURATIONS

ESTIMATE HOW LONG EACH ACTIVITY WILL TAKE TO COMPLETE

6.5 Estimate Activity Durations

Level of detail leads to accuracy

Activity lists

Activity resource requirements

Activity attributes

Resource capabilities

Organizational process assets

_____

_____

_____

_____

_____

_____

_____

ITTO: Estimate Activity Durations

Inputs	Tools & Techniques	Outputs
Schedule management plan	Expert judgment	Activity duration estimates
Activity list	Analogous estimating	Project documents updates
Activity attributes	Parametric estimating	
Activity resource requirements	Three-point estimating	
Resource calendars	Group decision-making techniques	
Project scope statement	Reserve analysis	
Risk register		
Resource breakdown structure		
Enterprise environmental factors		
Organizational process assets		

Analogous Estimating

Creates an analogy

Similar project work

Historical information

Top-down estimating

_____

_____

_____

_____

_____

_____

_____

Parametric Estimating

Parameter for estimating

Repetitive work

Learning curve

Three-Point Estimates

Finds an average of
- ◦ Optimistic
- ◦ Most likely
- ◦ Pessimistic
- ◦ Also called triangular distribution

(O+ML+P)/3=Estimate

(25+45+75)/3=48.33 hours

PERT Estimates

Program Evaluation and Review Technique

Also called beta distribution

$(O+(4ML)+P)/6 = estimate$

$(25+(4 \times 45)+75)/6 = 46.66$ hours

Reserve Time

Parkinson's Law

10-15 percent of project duration

Allotted to time overruns

DEVELOP THE PROJECT SCHEDULE

DEFINE WHEN THE PROJECT ACTIVITIES WILL TAKE PLACE – AND FIND FLOAT AND THE CRITICAL PATH

6.6 Develop Schedule

Defines the sequence of events

Durations of the activities and project

Determines when resources are needed

Establishes logical relationships between activities

_____

_____

_____

_____

_____

_____

_____

_____

ITTO: Develop Schedule

Inputs	Tools & Techniques	Outputs
Schedule management plan	Schedule network analysis	Schedule baseline
Activity list	Critical path method	Project schedule
Activity attributes	Critical chain method	Schedule data
Project schedule network diagrams	Resource optimization techniques	Project calendars
Activity resource requirements	Modeling techniques	PM plan updates
Resource calendars	Leads and lags	Project documents updates
Activity duration estimates	Schedule compression	
Project scope statement	Scheduling tool	
Risk register		
Project staff assignments		
Resource breakdown structure		
Enterprise environmental factors		
Organizational process assets		

Project Constraints

Must start on

Must finish on

Start no earlier than

Start no later than

Finish no earlier than

Finish no later than

Assumptions and Scheduling

New work

Risks

Force majeure

Labor

Effort

Risks and the Schedule

Risk is an uncertain event or condition

Knowns and unknowns

Risk analysis affects completion

Risk affects costs and time

_____

_____

_____

_____

_____

_____

_____

Determining the Project Timeline

PERT charts

Project calendars

Effort and efficiency

Alternative identifications

ID	Task Name	Duration	'97	28 Jul '97	4 Aug '97	11 Aug '97
			F S S	M T W T F S S	M T W T F S S	M T W T F S
1	Establish the need	2d				
2	Set target date	1d				
3	Establish leadtimes	1d				
4	Book venue	1d				
5	Choose advert location	1d				
6	Agree format	2d				
7	Devise tests	5d				
8	Job description	2d				
9	Set criteria	1d				
10	Write advert	2d				
11	Place advert	1d				
12	Shortlist	3d				
13	Invite candidates	1d				
14	Conduct interviews	3d				
15	Take decision	1d				
16						
17						

Project Network Diagram

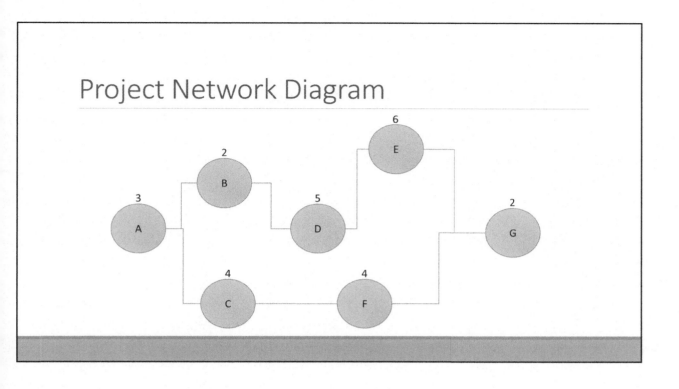

Schedule Network Analysis

Find earliest completion date

Find latest completion date

Find opportunities to shift resources

Find opportunities to delay

SWOT

Project Network Diagram

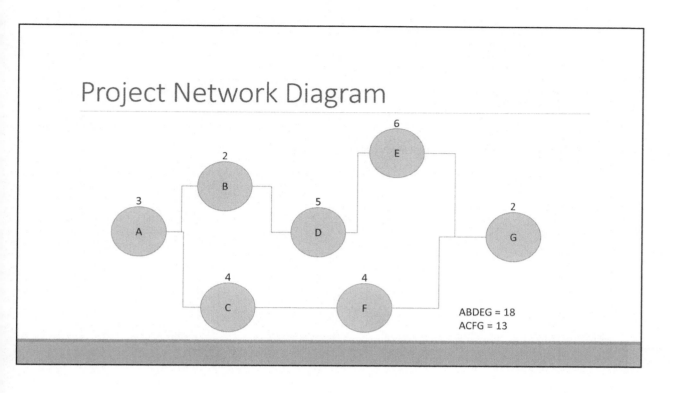

ABDEG = 18
ACFG = 13

Finding Float

Free float   An activity can be delayed without delaying the early start of any successor activities

Total float   An activity can be delayed without delaying project completion

Project float   A project can be delayed without passing the customer-expected completion date

Forward Pass: ES+du-1=EF

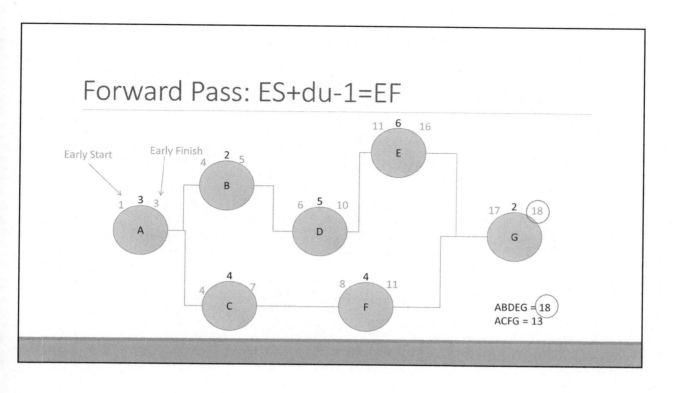

ABDEG = 18
ACFG = 13

Backward Pass: LF-du+1=LS

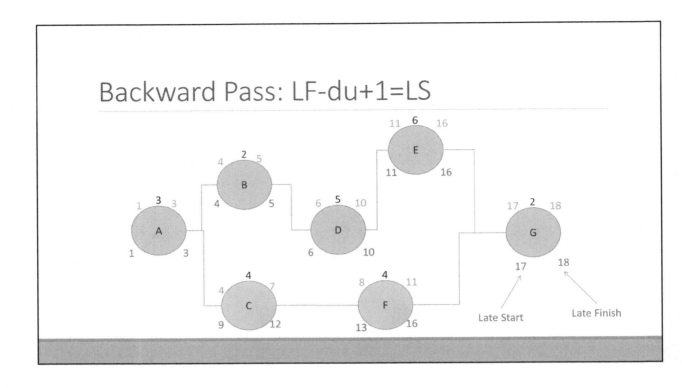

Backward Pass: LF-du+1=LS

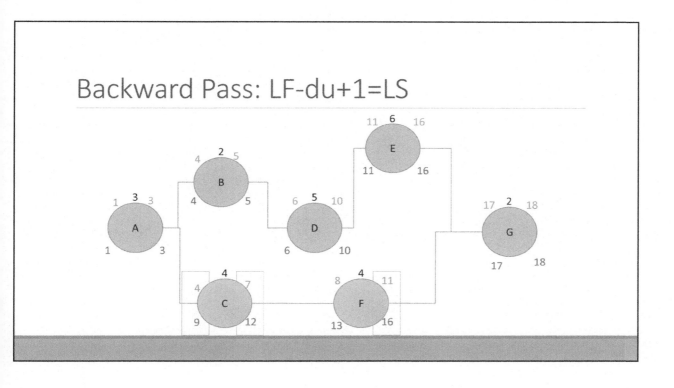

Practicing Float

Float Exercise worksheet

Create your own samples

Only a few questions on float

PRACTICE ACTIVITY

PRACTICE FINDING FLOAT AND THE CRITICAL PATH

_____

_____

_____

_____

_____

_____

_____

Activity: Practice Float

Float Questions

If activity E is delayed two days how much can activity G be delayed?

If the duration of activity D takes three additional days how long will the project take to finish?

If activity F takes 11 days to complete what is the earliest day that activity G will be able to finish?

Activity Answer: Practice Float

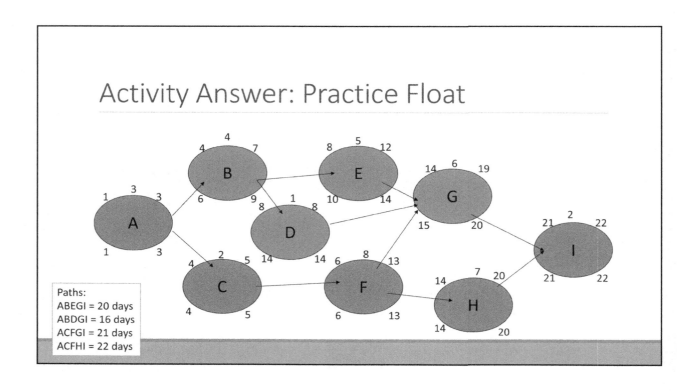

Paths:
ABEGI = 20 days
ABDGI = 16 days
ACFGI = 21 days
ACFHI = 22 days

Float Question Answers

If activity E is delayed two days how much can activity G be delayed?
- Zero! If Activity E is delayed two days then the path will equal 22 days in duration.

If the duration of activity D takes three additional days how long will the project take to finish?
- The project will still take 22 days total as there are six days of float available for Activity D.

If activity F takes 11 days to complete what is the earliest day that activity G will be able to finish?
- Activity G couldn't start until Day 17 and will last six days. The earliest Activity G could finish would be Day 22.

Using the Critical Chain Method

Focuses on project delivery date

Consider the availability of resources

Adds buffer on activities to account for unknowns and resources

Critical path doesn't consider if resources are available

CONSIDER RESOURCE AVAILABILITY FOR SCHEDULING

RESOURCE AVAILABILITY AFFECTS PROJECT DURATION AND PROJECT SCHEDULE COMPRESSION

_____

_____

_____

_____

_____

_____

_____

Using Resource Leveling Heuristics

Limits labor in time period

Often extends the project schedule

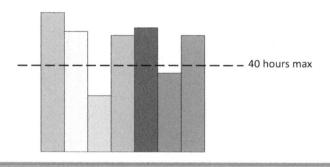

40 hours max

Schedule Compression

Crashing adds people and costs

Fast tracking adds risk and overlaps

Monte Carlo Simulation

Develop Schedule Process

Milestone charts

Bar charts

Project schedule network diagrams

Visualize the project work

_____

_____

_____

_____

_____

_____

_____

6.7 Control Schedule

Schedule Change Control System

Measuring project performance

Examining schedule variance

Updating the project schedule

Corrective actions

Lessons learned

ITTO: Control Schedule

Inputs	Tools & Techniques	Outputs
Project management plan	Performance reviews	Work performance information
Project schedule	Project management software	Schedule forecasts
Work performance data	Resource optimization techniques	Change requests
Project calendars	Modeling techniques	Project management plan updates
Schedule data	Leads and lags	Project documents updates
Organizational process assets	Schedule compression	Organizational process assets updates
	Scheduling tool	

Measuring Project Performance

Value tied to percentage of work completed

Planned value – what the project should be worth

Estimate to complete

Estimate at completion

Milestones

Key deliverables

Performance Reviews

Trend analysis

Critical path analysis

Critical chain method

Earned value management

Schedule forecasting

Learning Game!

http://www.instructing.com/wp-content/pub/6/story.html

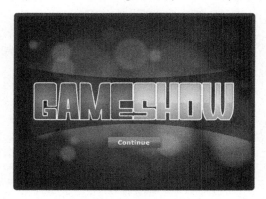

_____

_____

_____

_____

_____

_____

_____

Chapter exam

PLAN PROJECT COST MANAGEMENT

ESTIMATING, BUDGETING, AND CONTROLLING THE COSTS OF THE PROJECT

_____

_____

_____

_____

_____

_____

_____

_____

7.1 Plan Cost Management

Subsidiary plan of the project management plan

Addresses three cost management processes:
- How costs are estimates
- How the project budget is managed
- How costs will be controlled

ITTO: Plan Cost Management

Inputs	Tools & Techniques	Outputs
Project management plan	Expert judgment	Cost management plan
Project charter	Analytical techniques	
Enterprise environmental factors	Meetings	
Organizational process assets		

Cost Management Plan

Cost estimating approach

Budgeting approach

Cost control measures

Level of precision

Units of measure

Organizational procedure links

Control thresholds

Rules of performance measurement

Reporting formats

Process descriptions

ESTIMATE PROJECT COSTS

PROJECT COSTS MUST BE ESTIMATED BASED ON THE INFORMATION
AVAILABLE.

Estimating the Project Costs

Predictions based on current information

Cost tradeoffs and risks considered
- Cost versus buy
- Cost versus lease
- Sharing resources

Level of accuracy
- Rough order of magnitude estimate
- Budget estimate
- Definitive estimate

All categories of costs estimated

ITTO: Estimate Costs

Inputs	Tools & Techniques	Outputs
Cost management plan	Expert judgment	Activity cost estimates
HR management plan	Analogous estimating	Basis of estimates
Scope baseline	Parametric estimating	Project documents updates
Project schedule	Bottom-up estimating	
Risk register	Three-point estimating	
Enterprise environmental factors	Reserve analysis	
Organizational process assets	Cost of quality	
	Project management software	
	Vendor bid analysis	
	Group decision-making techniques	

Creating a Cost Estimate

Rough order of magnitude
- -25% to +75%

Budget estimate
- -10% to +25%

Definitive estimate
- -5% to +10%

Four Cost Categories

Direct costs

Indirect costs

Variable costs

Fixed costs

Project Schedule and Cost Estimating

Resource availability

Timing of procurement of resources

Cost of project financing

Time-sensitive costs

Seasonal cost variations

Analogous Estimating

Top down approach

Quick, but unreliable

Historical information

Project A

Project B

Parametric Estimating

Based on a cost parameter

$329 per software license

$4500 per metric ton

Consider the learning curve

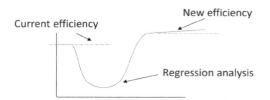

Current efficiency

New efficiency

Regression analysis

Bottom-Up Estimating

Based on WBS creation

Also called a definitive estimate

Cost of each work package

Cost of work packages are rolled-up

Three-Point Cost Estimates

Average of cost

(Optimistic + Most Likely + Pessimistic)/3

PERT

- (O+(4M)+P)/6

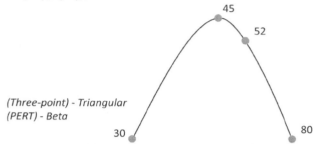

(Three-point) - Triangular
(PERT) - Beta

Vendor Bid Analysis

Should cost estimates (Third party estimates)

Statement of Work (SOW)

Bidders conference

Vendor selection
- Screening system
- Scoring model
- Price selection

Chapter 12, Procurement

Cost Estimate Results

Activity cost estimates

Basis of estimates
- Supporting detail
- Assumptions and constraints
- Range of variance
- Confidence level of estimate

CREATE THE PROJECT BUDGET

THE PROJECT BUDGET IS THE ACTUAL AMOUNT OF
FUNDS AVAILABLE FOR THE PROJECT EXPENSES

7.3 Determine Budget

Aggregating the estimated costs

Cost of work packages and activities

Authorized cost baseline

Excludes management reserves

Performance measured against budget

ITTO: Determine Budget

Inputs	Tools & Techniques	Outputs
Cost management plan	Cost aggregation	Cost baseline
Scope baseline	Reserve analysis	Project funding requirements
Activity cost estimates	Expert judgment	Project documents updates
Basis of estimates	Historical relationships	
Project schedule	Funding limit reconciliation	
Resource calendars		
Risk register		
Agreements		
Organizational process assets		

Reserve Analysis

Contingency reserve

Management reserve

Unknown unknowns

Not part of the cost baseline, but part of the project budget

Creating the Project Budget

Actual cost of the project

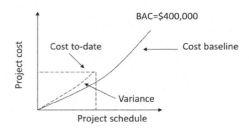

Relying on Historical Relationships

Both parametric and analogous are historical-based estimates

The historical information affects the estimates
- Accuracy of historical information
- Quantifiable parameters
- Models are scalable for any size project

Funding Limit Reconciliation

Reconcile planned and actual costs

Cost variances

Corrective actions

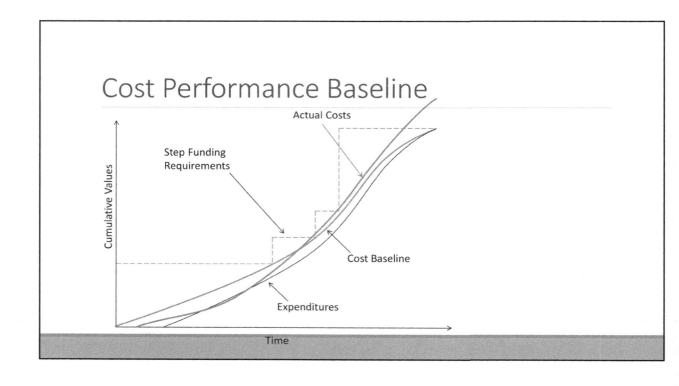

Project Funding Requirements

Total funding requirements

Periodic funding requirements

Anticipated liabilities

Management reserves

CONTROL PROJECT COST

COST MUST BE CONTROLLED WITHIN THE PROJECT AND CONSIDER CHANGES, ERRORS AND OMISSIONS, AND SHOW PROJECT PERFORMANCE

7.4 Control Costs

Monitoring status of the project

Managing changes to the cost baseline

Variance management and corrective actions

Balancing project risk and reward

Cost Control

Influence change factors

Change requests

Managing changes (approved/unapproved)

Tracking costs

Isolate variances for study

Earned value management

Communicating cost status

Cost overruns and allowed variances

ITTO: Control Costs

Inputs	Tools & Techniques	Outputs
Project management plan	Earned value management	Work performance information
Project funding requirements	Forecasting	Cost forecasts
Work performance data	To-complete performance index (TCPI)	Change requests
Organizational process assets	Performance reviews	Project management plan updates
	Project management software	Project documents updates
	Reserve analysis	Organizational process assets updates

Measuring Project Performance

Earned Value Management

Forecast

Measure performance

Suite of formulas

A few CAPM questions

EVM Foundation

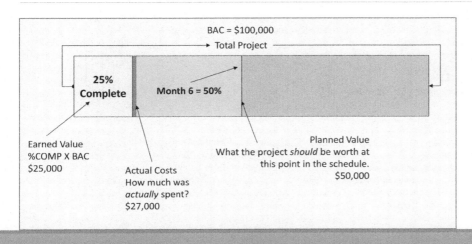

Finding the Variances

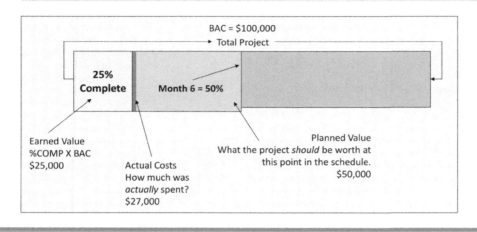

BAC = $100,000
Total Project

25% Complete

Month 6 = 50%

Earned Value
%COMP X BAC
$25,000

Actual Costs
How much was
actually spent?
$27,000

Planned Value
What the project *should* be worth at
this point in the schedule.
$50,000

Measuring Performance

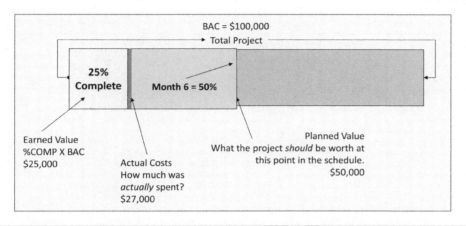

BAC = $100,000
Total Project

25% Complete

Month 6 = 50%

Earned Value
%COMP X BAC
$25,000

Actual Costs
How much was
actually spent?
$27,000

Planned Value
What the project *should* be worth at
this point in the schedule.
$50,000

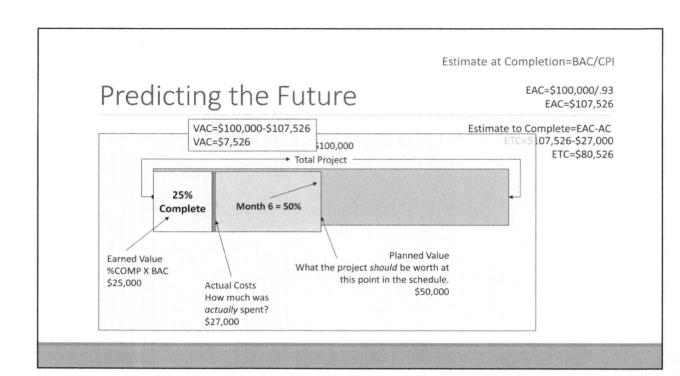

Predicting the Future

Estimate at Completion=BAC/CPI

EAC=$100,000/.93
EAC=$107,526

VAC=$100,000-$107,526
VAC=$7,526

Estimate to Complete=EAC-AC
ETC=$107,526-$27,000
ETC=$80,526

$100,000

Total Project

25% Complete

Month 6 = 50%

Earned Value
%COMP X BAC
$25,000

Actual Costs
How much was *actually* spent?
$27,000

Planned Value
What the project *should* be worth at this point in the schedule.
$50,000

To-Complete Performance Index

Can you meet the BAC?

Can you meet the EAC?

TCPI=(BAC-EV)/(BAC-AC)

TCPI=(BAC-EV)/(EAC-AC)

TCPI=(BAC-EV)/(BAC-AC)

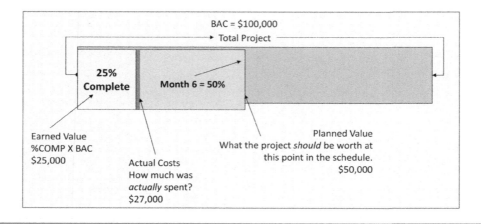

BAC = $100,000
→ Total Project

25% Complete

Month 6 = 50%

Earned Value
%COMP X BAC
$25,000

Actual Costs
How much was
actually spent?
$27,000

Planned Value
What the project *should* be worth at
this point in the schedule.
$50,000

330

TCPI=(BAC-EV)/(EAC-AC)

TCPI=($100,000-$25,000)/($107,526-$27,000)
TCPI=75,000/80,526
TCPI=.93

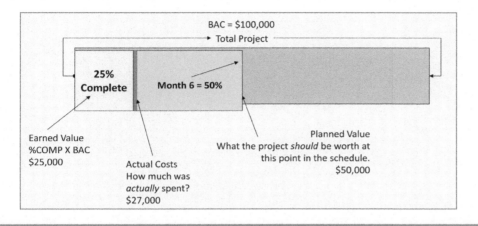

BAC = $100,000
Total Project

25% Complete

Month 6 = 50%

Earned Value
%COMP X BAC
$25,000

Actual Costs
How much was
actually spent?
$27,000

Planned Value
What the project *should* be worth at
this point in the schedule.
$50,000

Five EVM Rules

EV is first

Variance means subtract

Index means division

Less than one is bad in an index

Negative is bad in a variance

PRACTICE ACTIVITY

PRACTICE THE EARNED VALUE MANAGEMENT FORMULAS

Calculate for Earned Value Management

Consider that you are the project manager of the BGQ Project. This project has a budget of $1,560,000 and you are 30 percent complete. You are, however, supposed to be 35 percent complete today. In addition you've spent $512,000 to reach this point. Based on this information, solve for the following:

Earned value
Planned value
Cost variance
Schedule variance
Cost performance index
Schedule performance index

Estimate at completion
Estimate to complete
To-complete performance index (BAC)
To-complete performance index (EAC)
Variance at completion

Earned Value Management Answer

Consider that you are the project manager of the BGQ Project. This project has a budget of $1,560,000 and you are 30 percent complete. You are, however, supposed to be 35 percent complete today. In addition you've spent $512,000 to reach this point. Based on this information, solve for the following:

Earned value	468,000	Estimate at completion	1,706,667
Planned value	546,000	Estimate to complete	1,194,667
Cost variance	-44,000	To-complete performance index (BAC)	1.04
Schedule variance	-78,000	To-complete performance index (EAC)	0.91
Cost performance index	0.91	Variance at completion	-146,667
Schedule performance index	0.86		

Learning Game!

http://www.instructing.com/wp-content/pub/7/story.html

Chapter exam

_____

_____

_____

_____

_____

_____

_____

_____

_____

PLAN PROJECT QUALITY MANAGEMENT

PLANNING TO ACHIEVE QUALITY, PERFORMING QUALITY ASSURANCE AND QUALITY CONTROL WITHIN THE PROJECT

8.1 Plan Quality Management

Defines quality policy for the project

Defines quality assurance requirements

Defines how quality control activities will occur

ITTO: Plan Quality Management

Inputs	Tools & Techniques	Outputs
Project management plan	Cost-benefit analysis	Quality management plan
Stakeholder register	Cost of quality	Process improvement plan
Risk register	Seven basic quality tools	Quality metrics
Requirements documentation	Benchmarking	Quality checklists
Enterprise environmental factors	Design of experiments	Project documents updates
Organizational process assets	Statistical sampling	
	Additional quality planning tools	
	Meetings	

Quality Management Approach

Top-down quality

Beware of:
- Overworking the project team
- Speeding through quality inspections

Quality v. Grade

Quality is about fulfilling requirements
- Project scope
- Product scope
- Implied needs

Grade is a category or rank
- Class of services
- Types of materials

Quality and Grade

Low quality is always a problem, low grade may not be.

Accuracy and Precision and Quality

Precision is a measure of exactness.

Accuracy is an assessment of correctness.

Precise measurements aren't necessarily accurate measurements.

Accurate measurements aren't necessarily precise measurements.

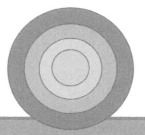

Quality Project Management

Customer satisfaction
- ◦ Conformance to requirements
- ◦ Fitness for use

Prevention
- ◦ "Quality is planned into a project, not inspected in."

Management responsibility

Deming's "Plan-Do-Check-Act"

Quality Project Management

Kaizen technologies
- ◦ Continuous small improvements to reduce costs and ensure consistency

Marginal analysis
- ◦ Study of the cost of improvements to a product or service and how the costs contribute to an increase in revenue
- ◦ Marginal costs to create one more unit

Determining the Quality Policy

Formal quality approaches
- ISO programs
- Six Sigma
- Total Quality Management

If a quality policy doesn't exists the project manager must create one for the project.

Standards and Regulations

Standards are optional

Regulations are requirements

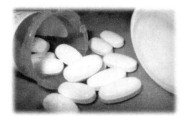 

Cost of Quality

Cost of conformance to requirements
- Safety measures
- Team development and training
- Proper materials and processes

Cost of non-conformance to requirements
- Liabilities, loss of life or limb
- Rework/scrap
- Lost business

USING SEVEN BASIC QUALITY TOOLS

THESE SEVEN TOOLS ARE USED FOR PROJECT QUALITY PLANNING, QUALITY ASSURANCE, AND QUALITY CONTROL

_____

_____

_____

_____

_____

_____

_____

_____

Seven Basic Quality Tools

Cause and effect diagrams

Flowcharts

Check sheets

Pareto Diagrams

Histograms

Control charts

Scatter diagrams

Cause and Effect Diagrams

Ishikawa or fishbone

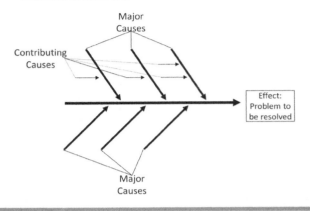

Flowcharting

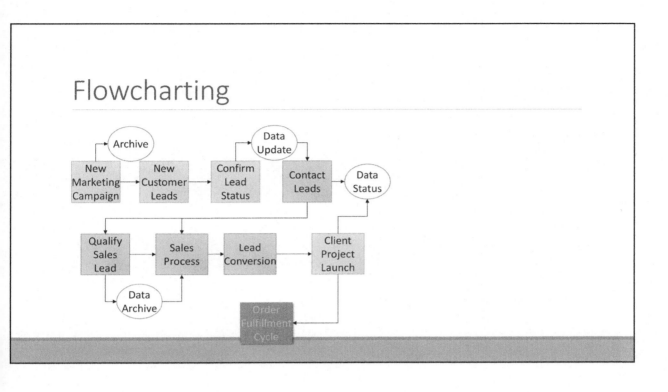

Pareto Chart

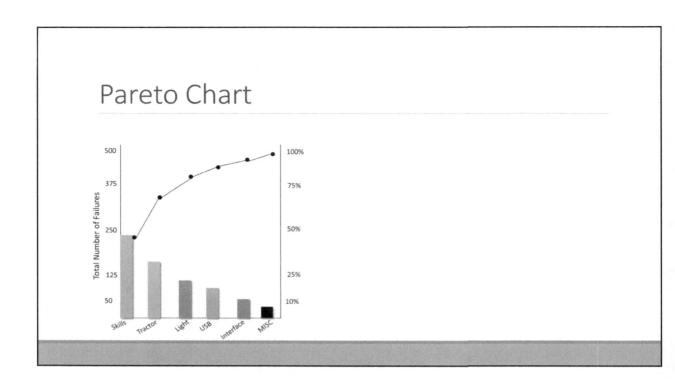

Histograms

Vertical bar chart show frequency

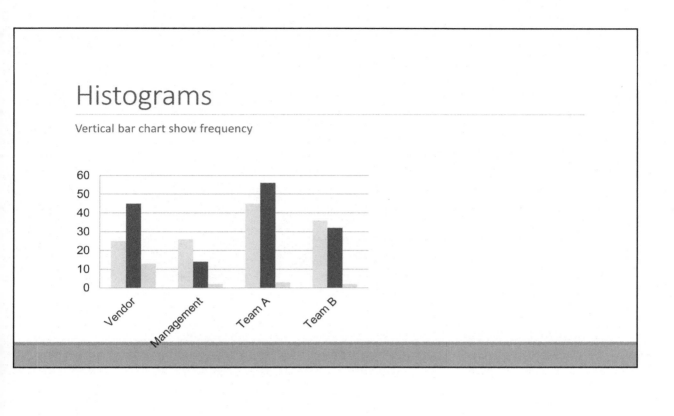

Control Charts

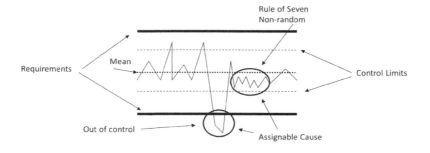

Control limits are usually ±3Σ

Creating a Scatter Diagram

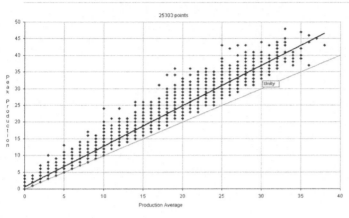

COMPLETE QUALITY MANAGEMENT PLANNING

PLANNING FOR QUALITY CREATES THE QUALITY
MANAGEMENT PLAN AND THE PROCESS IMPROVEMENT PLAN

Benchmarking the Project

Comparing two systems

Technology

Materials

Projects

Design of Experiments

Examines variables to determine the best outcome

One million postcards

The best results win

Quality Planning Tools

Brainstorming – generate ideas

Affinity diagrams – logical grouping of ideas

Force field analysis – forces for and against

Nominal group technique – small groups of brainstorming then ideas reviewed by a larger group

Quality Management Plan

Quality assurance

Quality control

Continuous process improvement

Operational definitions
- Terminology
- Metrics
- Lexicon/glossary

Process Improvement Plan

Process boundaries

Process configuration

Process metrics

Targets for improvement

PERFORM QUALITY ASSURANCE

QUALITY ASSURANCE IS DOING THE
WORK CORRECTLY THE FIRST TIME – WITH QUALITY

8.2 Perform Quality Assurance

Auditing the quality requirements

Auditing results of quality control

Facilitates improvement of quality processes

QA is prevention driven

Being certain about quality in the product

_____

_____

_____

_____

_____

_____

_____

_____

ITTO: Perform Quality Assurance

Inputs	Tools & Techniques	Outputs
Quality management plan	Quality management and control tools	Change requests
Process improvement plan	Quality audits	Project management plan updates
Quality metrics	Process analysis	Project documents updates
Quality control measurements		Organizational process assets updates
Project documents		

Quality Management and Control Tools

Affinity diagrams

Process decision program charts

Interrelationship diagraphs

Tree diagrams

Prioritization matrices

Activity network diagrams

Matrix diagrams

Completing a Quality Audit

Determine if project complies with organizational policies
- Best practices implemented?
- What nonconforming policies? What shortcomings?
- Share good practices with others?
- Offer assistance to improve processes?
- Highlight contributions?
- Lessons learned?

IMPLEMENT PROJECT QUALITY CONTROL

QUALITY CONTROL IS AN INSPECTION-DRIVEN ACTIVITY TO ENSURE THAT QUALITY EXISTS WITHIN THE PROJECT DELIVERABLES. ITS GOAL IS TO KEEP MISTAKES OUT OF THE HANDS OF THE CUSTOMER

8.3 Control Quality

Inspection-driven activity

Keep mistakes out of the customers' hands

Causal identification of poor quality

Validate quality for customer acceptance

ITTO: Control Quality

Inputs	Tools & Techniques	Outputs
Project management plan	Seven basic quality tools	Quality control measurements
Quality metrics	Statistical sampling	Validated changes
Quality checklists	Inspection	Validated deliverables
Work performance data	Approved change requests review	Work performance information
Approved change requests		Change requests
Deliverables		Project management plan updates
Project documents		Project documents updates
Organizational process assets		Organizational process assets updates

How to do Quality Control:

Inspect the project deliverables

Measure the work

Utilize the seven basic quality tools

Try statistical sampling

Learning Game!

http://www.instructing.com/wp-content/pub/3/story.html

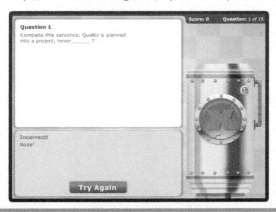

Chapter exam

PLAN PROJECT HUMAN RESOURCE MANAGEMENT

HOW TO MANAGE AND LEAD THE PEOPLE INVOLVED WITH THE PROJECT

_____

_____

_____

_____

_____

_____

_____

_____

9.1 Plan Human Resource Management

Identifying project team needs

Reporting relationships

Assigning roles and responsibilities

Staffing management plan
- Staff acquisition
- Release of staff
- Consideration of organizational policies and structure

ITTO: Plan Human Resource Management

Inputs	Tools & Techniques	Outputs
Project management plan	Organization charts and position descriptions	Human resource management plan
Activity resource requirements	Networking	
Enterprise environmental factors	Organizational theory	
Organizational process assets	Expert judgment	
	Meetings	

Organization Charts

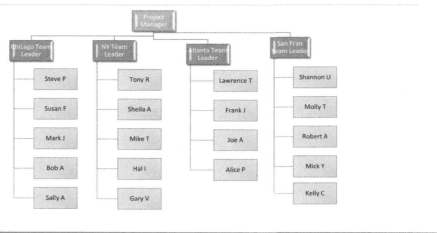

Matrix Chart

Activity	Team Member					
	Sam	Shelly	Ben	Frank	Lloyd	Mark
Web content	R	A		C	I	
Web design	A	R				
App development	I		A		R	
Security	I		R	I	I	A
Proofing				A		
Testing				R		
Payment system	I		I	I	I	R

Maslow's Hierarchy of Needs

Self-actualization

Esteem

Social

Safety

Physiological

Herzberg's Theory of Motivation

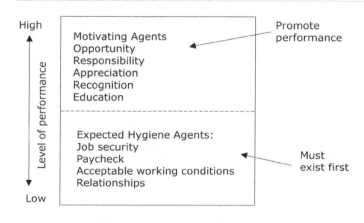

McGregor's X and Y

X People

Micromanagement
No trust
Lazy
Avoid work

Y People

Self-led
Motivated
Capable

McClelland's Theory of Needs

David McClelland's Acquired Needs Theory

Individual's needs are acquired over time

Shaped by life experiences
- Achievement – seeks to excel
- Affiliation – harmonious, acceptance
- Power – personal and institutional

Thematic Apperception Test (TAT)

Other Theories

Ouchi's Theory Z
- Japanese Management Style
- Lifelong employment

Expectancy Theory
- People behave based on what they believe their behavior will bring them

Halo effect
- False belief based on a person's experiences

DEFINE ROLES AND RESPONSIBILITIES

WHO DOES WHAT AND WHO DECIDES WHAT

_____

_____

_____

_____

_____

_____

_____

Organizational Planning

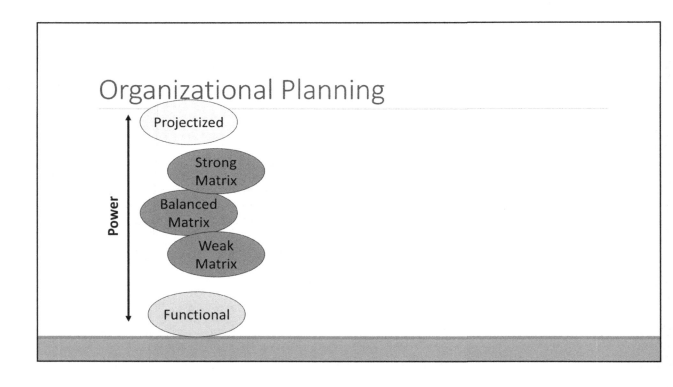

Roles and Responsibilities

Role – the label describing the portion of the project the person is accountable.

Authority – apply resources, make decisions, sign approvals.

Responsibility – the work that a project team member is expected to perform.

Competency – the skill and capacity required to complete project activities

Examining the Staffing Management Plan

Part of the human resource management plan

Staff acquisition

Resource calendars

Resource histogram

Staff release plan

Training needs

Recognition and rewards

Compliance and safety

ACQUIRE THE PROJECT TEAM

HOW WILL PEOPLE JOIN YOUR PROJECT TEAM?

_____

_____

_____

_____

_____

_____

_____

Acquiring the Project Team

Negotiate and influence

Wrong resources affect project's success

Alternate resources
- Costs
- Competency
- Training
- Legal, regulatory, or mandatory criteria

ITTO: Acquire Project team

Inputs	Tools & Techniques	Outputs
Human resource management plan	Pre-assignment	Project staff assignments
Enterprise environmental factors	Negotiation	Resource calendars
Organizational process assets	Acquisition	Project management plan updates
	Virtual teams	
	Multi-criteria decision analysis	

Acquiring the Project Team

Pre-assignment

Negotiation

Acquisition

Working with Virtual Teams

Geographically dispersed individuals

Experts in different geographical areas

Inclusion of workers from home offices

Project members with varying schedules

People with mobility handicaps

The deletion or reduction of travel expenses

Multi-Criteria Decision Analysis for Team

Availability

Costs

Experience

Ability

Knowledge

Skills

Attitude

International factors

Results of Team Acquisition

Project staff assignments

Resource calendars

Project management plan updates

LEAD PROJECT TEAM DEVELOPMENT

YOUR TEAM NEEDS TO WORK TOGETHER AND RELY ON ONE ANOTHER

9.3 Develop Project Team

Process to improve competencies

Promote team member interaction

Enhance overall project performance

Overall goals of this process:
- Improve teamwork
- Motivate employees
- Reduce turnover rate
- Improve overall project performance

ITTO: Develop Project Team

Inputs	Tools & Techniques	Outputs
Human resource management plan	Interpersonal skills	Team performance assessments
		Enterprise environmental factors updates
Project staff assignments	Training	
Resource calendars	Team-building activities	
	Ground rules	
	Colocation	
	Recognition and rewards	
	Personnel assessment tools	

Leading Team Development

Interpersonal skills – soft skills
- Communication
- Emotional intelligence
- Conflict resolution
- Influence

Training the project team

Team building activities

Forming, storming, norming, performing, and adjourning

Team Development, continued

Ground rules

Colocation – tight matrix

Recognition and rewards
- Money
- Throughout the project
- Avoid zero sum rewards

Personal assessment tools
- Attitudinal surveys
- Structured interviews

Team Performance Assessments

Improvements in skills

Team competency

Reduced staff turn over rate

Team cohesiveness

MANAGE THE PROJECT TEAM

MANAGING THE PROJECT TEAM TO GET PROJECT RESULTS

9.4 Manage Project Team

Tracking team member performance

Offering feedback to team members

Managing team changes

Influencing team behavior

Resolving conflict

ITTO: Manage Project Team

Inputs	Tools & Techniques	Outputs
Human resource management plan	Observation and conversation	Change requests
Project staff assignments	Project performance appraisals	Project management plan updates
Team performance assessments	Conflict management	Project documents updates
Issue log	Interpersonal skills	Enterprise environmental factors updates
Work performance reports		Organizational process assets updates
Organizational process assets		

Utilizing Organizational Process Assets

Organizational process assets can help manage the project team:
- Certificates of appreciation
- Newsletters
- Project websites
- Bonus structures
- Corporate apparel

Conflict Management

Conflict is natural

Team issue

Openness resolves conflict

Focus on issues, not personalities

Focus on present, not past

Managing Conflict

Relative importance of the conflict

Time pressure for conflict resolution

Positions of each person involved

Motivation to resolve conflict for short-term or long-term

Solving Problems

Withdrawal (avoiding)

Smoothing (accommodating)

Compromising

Forcing

Collaborating

Problem solving (confronting)

Relying on Interpersonal Skills

Leadership – aligning, motivating, inspiring

Influencing – organizational structure and authority
- Persuasive
- Active and effective listening
- Aware of project team interactions and issues
- Maintaining trust while also managing the project team

Making Effective Decisions

Focus on project goals

Follow a decision-making process

Study environmental factors

Analyze information

Develop personal qualities of project team members

Stimulate team creativity

Manage risk

Be approachable

Management Styles

Autocratic: The project manager makes all decisions

Democratic: The project team is involved with the decisions

Laissez Faire: the project manager allows the team to lead and make decisions

Exceptional: the project manager manages by exception (reactive)

Five Project Management Powers

Expert - experienced

Reward - incentive

Formal - positional

Coercive - threatened

Referent – references

Learning Game!

http://www.instructing.com/wp-content/pub/9/story.html

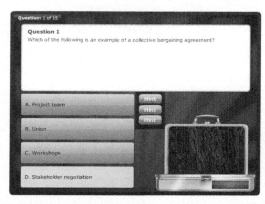

Chapter exam

PLAN PROJECT COMMUNICATIONS MANAGEMENT

COMMUNICATION IS 90% OF PROJECT MANAGEMENT

_____

_____

_____

_____

_____

_____

_____

_____

10.1 Plan Communications Management

Communication is paramount in project management

Creates project communications management plan

Defines how communication will be managed and controlled

Linked to stakeholder management and engagement

ITTO: Plan Communications Management

Inputs	Tools & Techniques	Outputs
Project management plan	Communication requirements analysis	Communications management plan
Stakeholder register	Communication technology	Project documents updates
Enterprise environmental factors	Communication models	
Organizational process assets	Communication methods	
	Meetings	

Who are stakeholders?

Persons and organizations

Involved in the project

Affected positively or negatively by project

Some can exert influence over the project

Stakeholder Register

Identification information

Assessment information

Stakeholder classification

Project Communications Management Planning

Who needs what information?

Who is authorized to access the information?

Who will provide the information?

When do they need it?

What modality?

Where will the information be stored?

Will time zones, language barriers, or cross-cultural issues affect the communication?

Communications Channel Formula

N(N-1)/2

10(10-1)/2

90/2=45

How many more communication channels?

Communication Requirements

Organization charts

Stakeholder responsibility relationships

Disciplines, departments, and specialties

Logistics of involvement

Internal and external communication needs

Stakeholder information

Communication Technology

Urgency of the need for information

Availability of technology

Ease of use

Project environment

Sensitivity and confidentiality of the information

Communication Model

Sender

Encoder

Medium

Decoder

Receiver

Noise

Barriers

Acknowledgements

Feedback/Response

Communication Methods

Interactive communication

Push communication

Pull communication

Communications Management Plan

Stakeholder communication requirements

Information to be communicated

Reason for the distribution

Time frame and frequency for the distribution

Person responsible for communicating the information

Person responsible for authorizing release of confidential information

Communications Management Plan

Methods or technologies

Resources allocated for communication activities

Escalation process

Method for updating and refining the communications management plan

Glossary of common terminology

Flow charts of the information flow in the project

Communication constraints

MANAGE PROJECT COMMUNICATIONS

MANAGING THE DAY-TO-DAY EFFORT OF THE PROJECT COMMUNICATIONS

ITTO: Manage Communications

Following the communications management plan to:
- Create
- Collect
- Store
- Distribute
- Retrieve

Ensures flow of communication among project stakeholders

ITTO: Manage Communications

Inputs	Tools & Techniques	Outputs
Communications management plan	Communication technology	Project communications
Work performance reports	Communication models	Project management plan updates
Enterprise environmental factors	Communication methods	Project documents updates
Organizational process assets	Information management systems	Organizational process assets updates
	Performance reporting	

Information Distribution Techniques

Sender-receiver models

Choice of media

Writing style

Meeting management techniques

Facilitation techniques

Using an Information Management System

Hard copy documents: memos, letters, reports, press releases

Electronic communications: email, fax, voice, video and web conferences, websites, web publishing

Electronic project management tools: web software, project management software, virtual office support, collaborative tools

Performance Reports

Prior to project meetings

Forecasting
- ◦ Estimate to Complete
- ◦ Estimate at Completion

Analogy to other projects (benchmarking)

Work re-estimation

External events impact

Results of Information Distribution

Stakeholder notifications

Project reports

Project presentations

Project records

Feedback from stakeholders

Lessons learned

CONTROL PROJECT COMMUNICATIONS

ENSURING THAT THE PROJECT COMMUNICATIONS MANAGEMENT PLAN IS FOLLOWED

10.3 Control Communications

Right information, right parties, at the right time

Follows and enforces communications management plan

Ensures optimal information flow among the parties

ITTO: Control Communications

Inputs	Tools & Techniques	Outputs
Project management plan	Information management systems	Work performance information
Project communications	Expert judgment	Change requests
Issue log	Meetings	Project management plan updates
Work performance data		Project documents updates
Organizational process assets		Organizational process assets updates

Controlling Communications

Information management systems

Relying on expert judgment
- Leaders in the organization
- Consultants
- Subject matter experts
- PMO

Meetings

Performance Reports

Status reports

Progress measurements

Forecasts

Baseline to actual comparisons

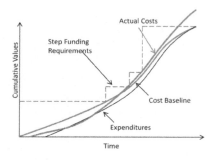

Forecasting Methods

Time series method
- Earned value
- Moving average
- Extrapolation
- Linear prediction
- Trend estimation
- Growth curve

Judgmental methods
- Intuitive judgments
- Opinions
- Probability

Forecasting Methods

Casual/econometric methods
- Causal factors for experiences
- Linear regression
- Autoregressive moving average (ARMA)
- Econometrics

Other methods...
- Simulation
- Probabilistic forecasting
- Ensemble forecasting

Learning Game!

http://www.instructing.com/wp-content/pub/10/story.html

Chapter exam

_____

_____

_____

_____

_____

_____

_____

_____

PLAN PROJECT RISK MANAGEMENT

PLANNING, ANALYZING, RESPONDING TO, AND CONTROLLING
PROJECT RISKS

What is risk?

Risk and reward

Risk is not always bad

Business risks

Pure risks

Planning for Risk Management

Risk appetite

Risk tolerance

Risk threshold

Stakeholder tolerance

Utility function

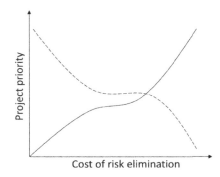

11.1 Plan Risk Management

Defines how risk management activities will occur

Risk activities in relation to project importance

Defines how the key stakeholders will:
- Identify risks
- Analyze risks
- Create risk responses
- Control risks

ITTO: Plan Risk Management

Inputs	Tools & Techniques	Outputs
Project management plan	Analytical techniques	Risk management plan
Project charter	Expert judgment	
Stakeholder register	Meetings	
Enterprise environmental factors		
Organizational process assets		

Planning Meetings and Analysis

Project manager, project team, stakeholders

Cost elements

Schedule activities

Risk management plan

Relying on Risk Management Policies

Enterprise environmental factors

Nature of the work

Industry standards

Regulated policies

Creating a Risk Management Plan

Methodology

Roles and responsibilities

Budgeting

Timing

Risk categories

Creating a Risk Management Plan

Definitions of risk probability and impact

Probability and impact matrix

Stakeholder tolerances

Reporting formats

Tracking

IDENTIFY PROJECT RISK

ALWAYS BE ON THE LOOKOUT FOR NEW RISK EVENTS – FROM START TO FINISH

Risk Categories

Risk Breakdown Structure

Technical, quality, or performance risks

Project management risks

Organization risks

External risks

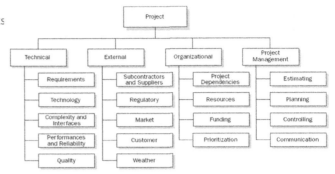

11.2 Identify Risks

Identifying and documenting risks

Creates a risk register

Ongoing activity throughout the project

ITTO: Identify Risks

Inputs	Tools & Techniques	Outputs
Risk management plan	Documentation reviews	Risk register
Cost management plan	Information gathering techniques	
Schedule management plan	Checklist analysis	
Quality management plan	Assumptions analysis	
Human resource management plan	Diagramming techniques	
Scope baseline	SWOT analysis	
Activity cost estimates	Expert judgment	
Activity duration estimates		
Stakeholder register		
Project documents		
Procurement documents		
Enterprise environmental factors		
Organizational process assets		

Information Gathering Techniques

Brainstorming

Delphi Technique

Checklists

Assumptions analysis

Diagramming Techniques

SWOT

Expert judgment

Creating a Risk Register

Central risk repository

Identified risks

Potential responses

Root cause

Risk categories

Risk status

PERFORM PROJECT RISK ANALYSIS

ANALYZING THE RISK EVENTS FOR PROBABILITY AND IMPACT ON PROJECT SUCCESS

_____

_____

_____

_____

_____

_____

_____

11.3 Perform Qualitative Risk Analysis

Fast, subjective approach to analysis

Qualify the risk for more analysis

Can be done as risks are identified

Cardinal or ordinal scale

ITTO: Perform Qualitative Risk Analysis

Inputs	Tools & Techniques	Outputs
		Project documents updates
Risk management plan	Risk probability and impact assessment	
Scope baseline	Probability and impact matrix	
Risk register	Risk data quality assessment	
Enterprise environmental factors	Risk categorization	
Organizational process assets	Risk urgency assessment	
	Expert judgment	

Probability-Impact Matrix

Odds and Impact

Risk	Probability	Impact	Risk Score
Data loss	Low	High	Moderate
Network speed	Moderate	Moderate	Moderate
Server downtime	High	Low	Moderate
Email service down	Low	Low	Low

Each identified risk

Subjective score

Other Qualitative Tools

Risk Data Quality Assessment

Risk Categorization

Risk Urgency Assessment

Expert judgment

11.4 Perform Quantitative Risk Analysis

Quantifying the identified risks

Usually for the more serious risks
- Probability
- Impact

Helps with decision-making for risk response

ITTO: Perform Quantitative Risk Analysis

Inputs	Tools & Techniques	Outputs
Risk management plan	Data gathering and representation techniques	Project documents updates
Cost management plan	Quantitative risk analysis and modeling techniques	
Schedule management plan	Expert judgment	
Risk register		
Enterprise environmental factors		
Organizational process assets		

Goals of Quantitative Analysis

Likelihood of reaching project success

Likelihood of reaching a project objective

Project's risk exposure

Contingency reserve

Identify the risks with the largest impact

Determine realistic time, cost, and scope targets

Performing Quantitative Analysis

Interviewing stakeholders and experts

Risk distributions

Sensitivity analysis

Expected Monetary Value

Modeling and simulation

Expert judgment

Using Sensitivity Analysis

Identifies the risks with most potential impact on the project

Measures and examines uncertainties

Tornado diagram often used with sensitivity analysis

Probability-Impact Matrix

Cardinal scale

Risk exposure

Sum of contingency reserve

"Hedging bets"

Probability-Impact Matrix

Risk event	Probability	Impact	Ex$V
A	.60	-10,000	-6,000
B	.20	-75,000	-15,000
C	.10	25,000	2,500
D	.40	-85,000	-34,000

Contingency reserve = $52,500

Examining the Results of Quantitative Risk Analysis

Probabilistic analysis of the project

Probability of achieving time and cost objectives

Prioritized list of quantified risks

Trends in quantitative risk analysis results

CREATE PROJECT RISK RESPONSES

THERE ARE SEVEN RISK RESPONSES FOR
RISK EVENTS WITHIN A PROJECT

11.5 Plan Risk Responses

Enhance opportunities

Reduce risks

Documents risk responses

Tracks outcomes for lessons learned

ITTO: Plan Risk Responses

Inputs	Tools & Techniques	Outputs
Risk management plan	Strategies for negative risks or threats	Project management plan updates
Risk register	Strategies for positive risks or opportunities	Project documents updates
	Contingent response strategies	
	Expert judgment	

Responding to Negative Risks

Avoidance

Transference

Mitigation

Managing Positive Risks

Exploiting

Sharing

Enhancing

Managing Positive and Negative Risks

Acceptance
- Laws
- Constraints
- Discounts
- Weather
- Force Majeure

Contingent Responses

When certain events occur

Certain predefined conditions

Triggers

Risk registers

Risk Register Updates

Risks, owners, responsibilities

Response strategies

Triggers, warning signs, conditions

Contingency plans

Fallback plans

Managing Risks

Residual risks

Secondary risks

Risk response contracts

Justifying risk reduction

CONTROL PROJECT RISK

CONTROLLING PROJECT RISKS TO MINIMIZE THREATS AND MAXIMIZE OPPORTUNITIES

Control Risks

Implementing risk response plans

Tracking identified risks

Monitoring residual risks

Evaluating risk process effectiveness

ITTO: Control Risks

Inputs	Tools & Techniques	Outputs
Project management plan	Risk reassessment	Work performance information
Risk register	Risk audits	Change requests
Work performance data	Variance and trend analysis	Project management plan updates
Work performance reports	Technical performance measurement	Project documents updates
	Reserve analysis	Organizational process assets updates
	Meetings	

Risk Monitoring and Control

Risk reassessment

Risk audits

Variance and trend analysis

Technical performance information

Reserve analysis

Status meetings

Results of Monitoring and Control

Work performance information

Change requests
- Corrective actions
- Preventive actions

Project management plan updates

Project document updates

Organizational process assets

Learning Game!

http://www.instructing.com/wp-content/pub/11/story.html

Chapter exam

_____

_____

_____

_____

_____

_____

_____

_____

PLAN PROJECT PROCUREMENT MANAGEMENT

PLANNING FOR PROCUREMENT, WORKING WITH CONTRACTS, CONTROLLING PROCUREMENT ACTIVITIES, AND CLOSING OUT PROCUREMENT

12.1 Plan Procurement Management

Documents the procurement approach

Defines the procurement decisions

Identifies potential sellers

Approach for acquiring resources and services

ITTO: Plan Procurement Management

Inputs	Tools & Techniques	Outputs
Project management plan	Make-or-buy analysis	Procurement management plan
Requirements documentation	Expert judgment	Procurement statement of work
Risk register	Market research	Procurement documents
Activity resource requirements	Meetings	Source selection criteria
Project schedule		Make-or-buy decisions
Activity cost estimates		Change requests
Stakeholder register		Project documents updates
Enterprise environmental factors		
Organizational process assets		

Procurement Management Plan

Type of contracts to be used

Risk management issues

Independent estimates

Organizational procurement procedures

Procurement documents

Managing multiple suppliers

Procurement Management Plan

Coordinating procurement activities

Constraints and assumptions

Required procurement lead time

Make or buy decisions

Scheduling deliverables in the contract

Performance bonds, insurance

Procurement Management Plan

WBS provided by seller

Form and format for SOW documents

Identifying pre-qualified sellers

Procurement metrics for evaluations

Source Selection Criteria

Understanding of need

Life cycle cost

Technical capability

Risk

Management approach

Technical approach

Warranty

Financial capacity

Production capacity and interest

Business size and type

Past performance of sellers

References

Intellectual property rights

Proprietary rights

Procurement Overview

Buyer is a stakeholder for seller

Seller is the project management team

Terms and conditions of contract for seller

External and internal "contracts"

Evaluating the Market Conditions

Sole source

Single source

Oligopoly

REVIEW PROJECT PROCUREMENT CONTRACTS

KNOW THESE CONTRACT TYPES AND THEIR CHARACTERISTICS FOR
THE CAPM EXAM

All About Contracts

A contract is a formal agreement

The United States backs all contracts through the court system

Contracts state all requirements for product acceptance

Changes to the contract must be formally approved, controlled, and documented

Contracts can be used as a risk mitigation tool

Contract Legalities

Fixed Price or Cost Reimbursable

Contain an offer

Have been accepted

Provide for a consideration (payment)

Be for a legal purpose

Be executed by someone with capacity and authority

Firm Fixed-Price Contracts (FFP)

Most common contract

Seller carries risk of cost overruns

Buyer specifies what's to be purchased

Changes to the scope

Fixed-Price Incentive Fee Contracts (FPIF)

Financial incentives for performance

Cost, schedule, technical performance

Price ceiling

Seller carries risk of overruns

Fixed Price with Economic Price Adjustment Contracts (FP-EPA)

Long-term contracts

Pre-defined financial adjustments

Inflation, cost increases, decreases

External conditions

Cost Reimbursable Overview

Cost plus a fee

Scope of work can't be defined early

High risks may exists in the project

Buyer carries risk of overruns

Cost Plus Fixed Fee Contracts (CPFF)

All allowable costs

Fixed fee of the initial estimated costs

Fee paid for completed work

Fee is constant unless scope changes

Cost Plus Incentive Fee (CPIF)

All allowable costs

Fee based on performance goals

Incentive sharing (often 80/20)

Contract defines measurements

Cost Plus Award Fee Contract (CPAF)

All allowable costs

Performance criteria for fee to seller

Subjective review by buyer

Award is determined by the buyer

Time and Materials Contract (T&M)

Seller is paid an hourly fee

Seller is paid for materials

Not-to-exceed clause

Time limits for contract

DECIDE TO BUILD OR TO BUY IN PROJECTS

A MATHEMATICAL ANALYSIS OF BUYING OR BUILDING A PROJECT SOLUTION

_____

_____

_____

_____

_____

_____

_____

Reasons to Buy or Build

Less costly

Use in-house skills

Control of work

Control of intellectual property

Learn new skills

Available staff

Focus on core project work

Build v. Buy Decisions

Build $65,000	Buy $52,000	Difference Buy v. Build $13,000
Build Monthly Fees $8,500	Buy Monthly Fees $10,500	Difference Monthly Fees $2,000

Divide Differences
$13,000/$2,000 = 6.5 months

PRACTICE ACTIVITY

PRACTICE THE BUY OR BUILD DETERMINATION

_____

_____

_____

_____

_____

_____

_____

_____

Determine to Build or Buy

Your team can create a solution for $245,600 and it will cost $23,500 per month to support. A vendor promises that you can purchase their solution for $12,000, but you'll have a monthly fee of $49,000. When could your solution be a better financial decision than the vendor's offer?

Build	Buy	Difference Buy v. Build

Build Monthly Fees	Buy Monthly Fees	Difference Monthly Fees

Divide Differences

_____

_____

_____

_____

_____

_____

_____

Answer: Determine to Build or Buy

Your team can create a solution for $245,600 and it will cost $23,500 per month to support. A vendor promises that you can purchase their solution for $12,000, but you'll have a monthly fee of $49,000. When could your solution be a better financial decision than the vendor's offer?

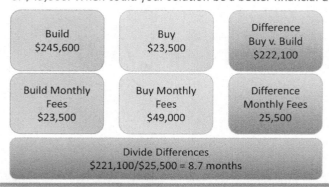

Build
$245,600

Buy
$23,500

Difference
Buy v. Build
$222,100

Build Monthly
Fees
$23,500

Buy Monthly
Fees
$49,000

Difference
Monthly Fees
25,500

Divide Differences
$221,100/$25,500 = 8.7 months

EXECUTE THE PROJECT PROCUREMENT MANAGEMENT PLAN

PROCURING GOODS AND SERVICES FOR THE PROJECT

_____

_____

_____

_____

_____

_____

_____

12.2 Conduct Procurements

Obtaining seller responses

Selecting the seller

Award a contract

ITTO: Conduct Procurements

Inputs	Tools & Techniques	Outputs
Procurement management plan	Bidder conference	Selected sellers
Procurement documents	Proposal evaluation techniques	Agreements
Source selection criteria	Independent estimates	Resource calendars
Seller proposals	Expert judgment	Change requests
Project documents	Advertising	Project management plan updates
Make-or-buy decisions	Analytical techniques	Project documents updates
Procurement statement of work	Procurement negotiations	
Organizational process assets		

Procurement Details

Qualified seller lists

Bidder conferences

Advertising

SOW updates

From the Buyer

SOW

Request for Quote

Invitation for Bid

Request for Proposal

Request for Information

From the Seller

Quote

Bid

Information

Proposal

Seller Selection

Weighting system

Independent estimates

Screening systems

Contract negotiation

Seller rating systems

Expert judgment

Proposal evaluation

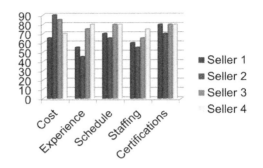

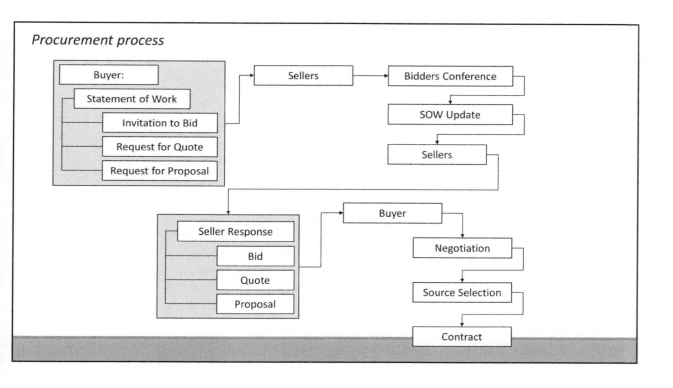

Procurement process

Buyer:
- Statement of Work
- Invitation to Bid
- Request for Quote
- Request for Proposal

Sellers → Bidders Conference → SOW Update → Sellers

Seller Response
- Bid
- Quote
- Proposal

Buyer → Negotiation → Source Selection → Contract

Contract Details (Agreement)

SOW and/or deliverables

Schedule baseline

Performance reporting

Period of performance

Roles and Responsibilities

Where work is to occur

Pricing

Payment terms

Inspection and acceptance criteria

Warranty

Product support

Limitation of liability

Fees and retainage

Penalties

Incentives

Insurance and performance bonds

Subordinate subcontractor approvals

Change request handling

Termination/alternative dispute resolution

CONTROL PROJECT PROCUREMENT

BOTH PARTIES MUST ABIDE BY THE TERMS OF THE CONTRACT

12.3 Control Procurements

Managing procurement relationships

Monitoring contract performance

Making changes and corrections to contract as needed

You could be the buyer or seller on the exam...

ITTO: Control Procurements

Inputs	Tools & Techniques	Outputs
Project management plan	Contract change control system	Work performance information
Procurement documents	Procurement performance reviews	Change requests
Agreements	Inspections and audits	Project management plan updates
Approved change requests	Payment systems	Project documents updates
Work performance reports	Claims administration	Organizational process assets updates
Work performance data	Records management system	
	Performance reporting	

Procurement and Processes

Direct and manage project execution

Report performance

Perform quality control

Perform integrated change control

Monitor and control risks

Administer Procurement Details

Payments to the seller

Seller compensation linked to progress

Seller performance review

Consideration for future assignments

Performing Contract Administration

Contract change control system

Buyer-conducted performance reviews and audits

Performance reporting

Payment system

Records management system

Claims Administration

Claims, disputes, or appeals

Contested changes

Disagreements

Terms of the contract

Alternative dispute resolution (ADR)

Negotiation is preferred method

CLOSE PROJECT PROCUREMENT

CLOSING PROCUREMENT IS ONE OF TWO PROJECT CLOSING PROCESSES

12.4 Close Procurements

Completing the procurement

Updating records to show results

Archiving contract information

Unresolved claims and litigation

Early termination
- Mutual agreement
- Default of one party
- Convenience of buyer (contractual)

ITTO: Close Procurements

Inputs	Tools & Techniques	Outputs
Project management plan	Procurement audits	Closed procurements
Procurement documents	Procurement negotiations	Organizational process assets updates
	Records management system	

Negotiated Settlements

Equitable settlement of all outstanding
- Issues
- Disputes
- Claims
- Difference of opinion

Mediation or arbitration

Litigation in the courts

Close Procurement Outputs

Formal written notice

Procurement file

Deliverable acceptance and signoff

Lessons learned documentation

_____

_____

_____

_____

_____

_____

_____

Learning Game!

http://www.instructing.com/wp-content/pub/12/story.html

Planning	Contracts	Documents	Sellers	Buy it?
100	100	100	100	100
300	300	300	300	300
500	500	500	500	500

_____

_____

_____

_____

_____

_____

_____

_____

Chapter exam

IDENTIFY PROJECT STAKEHOLDERS

IDENTIFYING, ENGAGING, AND MANAGING PROJECT STAKEHOLDERS

13.1 Identify Stakeholders

Identifying the people, groups, organizations

Documenting stakeholder information

Defining how the stakeholders could affect the project

New knowledge area in PMBOK Guide, fifth edition

_____

_____

_____

_____

_____

_____

_____

_____

ITTO: Identify Project Stakeholders

Inputs	Tools & Techniques	Outputs
Project charter	Stakeholder analysis	Stakeholder register
Procurement documents	Expert judgment	
Enterprise environmental factors	Meetings	
Organizational process assets		

Who are stakeholders?

Persons and organizations

Involved in the project

Affected positively or negatively by project

Some can exert influence over the project

Identifying Project Stakeholders

People and groups affected by the project

Stakeholder exert influence over the project

Identify early in the project

Stakeholder management strategy

Classify stakeholders according to:
- Interest
- Influence
- Involvement

Stakeholder Analysis

Identify all potential stakeholders and info

Key stakeholders are

- Decision-making role
- Management role
- Primary customer

Interview stakeholders
to identify stakeholders

Stakeholder Analysis

Power/Interest Grid

Power/Influence Grid

Influence/Impact Grid

Salience model
- Power
- Urgency
- Legitimacy

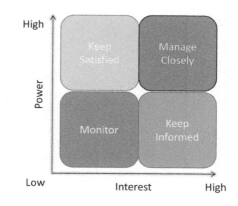

Stakeholder Register

Identification information

Assessment information

Stakeholder classification

PLAN STAKEHOLDER MANAGEMENT

CREATING A PLAN TO IDENTIFY, MANAGEMENT, AND ENGAGE STAKEHOLDERS

_____

_____

_____

_____

_____

_____

_____

13.2 Plan Stakeholder Management

Developing management strategies for stakeholder engagement

Analysis of stakeholder needs

Creates a clear plan for managing the stakeholders

ITTO: Plan Stakeholder Management

Inputs	Tools & Techniques	Outputs
Project management plan	Expert judgment	Stakeholder management plan
Stakeholder register	Meetings	Project documents updates
Enterprise environmental factors	Analytical techniques	
Organizational process assets		

Planning Stakeholder Management

Expert judgment for stakeholder management planning
- Senior management
- Project team members
- Organizational resources
- Identified key stakeholders
- Project managers
- Subject matter experts
- Regulatory bodies and nongovernmental agencies

Stakeholder Engagement Levels

Unaware

Resistant

Neutral

Supportive

Leading

Reviewing the Stakeholder Management Plan

Desired and current engagement levels

Scope and impact of change to stakeholders

Identified interrelationships and potential overlap

Stakeholder communication requirements

Information to be distributed

Reason for the distribution of that information

Time frame and frequency for the distribution of required information

MANAGE PROJECT STAKEHOLDER ENGAGEMENT

KEEPING STAKEHOLDERS ENGAGED IN THE PROJECT

13.3 Manage Stakeholder Engagement

Engaging stakeholders as needed in the project

Obtain, confirm, maintain stakeholder commitment to project

Manage stakeholder expectations

Address potential concerns

Clarifying and resolving issues

ITTO: Manage Stakeholder Engagement

Inputs	Tools & Techniques	Outputs
Stakeholder management plan	Communication methods	Issue log
Communications management plan	Interpersonal skills	Change requests
Change log	Management skills	Project management plan updates
Organizational process assets		Project documents updates
		Organizational process assets updates

Methods to Engage Stakeholders

Communication methods

Interpersonal skills
- Building trust
- Resolving conflict
- Active listening
- Overcoming resistance to change

Management skills
- Facilitate consensus
- Influence people
- Negotiate agreements
- "Modify organizational behavior to accept the project outcomes"

13.4 Control Stakeholder Engagement

Monitoring overall stakeholder relationships

Adjusting stakeholder management strategies

Updating stakeholder management plan as needed

Approach evolves as project continues

ITTO: Control Stakeholder Engagement

Inputs	Tools & Techniques	Outputs
Project management plan	Information management systems	Work performance information
Issue log	Expert judgment	Change requests
Work performance data	Meetings	Project management plan updates
Project documents		Project documents updates
		Organizational process assets updates

Actively Engaging Stakeholders

Relying on information management system

Using expert judgment

Meeting with stakeholders

Being honest and direct with project news

Learning Game!

http://www.instructing.com/wp-content/pub/13/story.html

Chapter exam

_____

_____

_____

_____

_____

_____

_____

_____

_____

ADHERE TO ETHICAL STANDARDS

PMI CODE OF ETHICS
AND PROFESSIONAL CONDUCT

PMI Code of Ethics and Professional Conduct

PMI document that is part of all PMI certification applications

Must agree to its terms

Available through www.pmi.org

Responsibilities to the Profession

Organizational rules and policies
- Exam application
- Test items
- Answer sheets
- Continuing certification reporting (PDUs)

Responsibilities to the Profession

Clear and factual evidence:
- Report violations
- Cooperate with PMI on their queries
- Disclose appearance of conflict of interest

Professional Practice

Truth in advertising and sales

Comply with laws, regulations, ethical standards of country where project management is held

Advancement of Profession

Intellectual property

Disperse the code

Responsibility to Customers and to the Public

Qualifications and experience
- Truthful in experience
- Truthful in estimates (no sandbagging)

Customer is in charge

Confidentiality (privity)

Responsibility to Customers and to the Public

Avoid Conflict of Interest

Refrain from accepting inappropriate compensation
- Follow the laws and customs of the country

Code of Conduct Extras

Sapir-Whorf Hypotheses
- understand the language

Culture shock
- Initial reaction to foreign environment

Ethnocentrism
- Measure other cultures by your own

Exam Tips

Laws of the country

Company policies

Customs

Ethics

Be an angel

What now?

Follow your study strategy

Practice your flashcards

Memorize the Memory Sheets

For additional training visit www.instructing.com

Made in the USA
Coppell, TX
25 March 2021

52357797R00313